GOING
to the
NEXT LEVEL

ELLIS D. POWELL

CREATION
HOUSE
A STRANG COMPANY

GOING TO THE NEXT LEVEL
by Ellis D. Powell
Published by Creation House
A Strang Company
600 Rinehart Road
Lake Mary, Florida 32746
www.creationhouse.com

Scripture quotations marked NKJV are from the New King James Version of the Bible. Copyright © 1979, 1980, 1982 by Thomas Nelson, Inc., publishers. Used by permission.

Scripture quotations marked KJV are from the King James Version of the Bible.

Scripture quotations marked NIV are from the Holy Bible, New International Version. Copyright © 1973, 1978, 1984, International Bible Society. Used by permission.

Cover design by Terry Clifton

Library of Congress Control Number: 2006926081
International Standard Book Number:
1-59979-015-7—Paperback Edition
1-59979-023-8—Hardback Edition

06 07 08 09 10 — 9 8 7 6 5 4 3 2 1
Printed in the United States of America

Dedication

My wife (true rib from my side), Karen Rochelle Powell. Thanks for always believing in me, truly being my helpmate, and always having my best interest in mind. Thanks, partner.

My daughters, Prenesha and Elexis, and son, Ellison (my seeds from my tree). May your lives be prosperous and bring forth fruit because your lives have truly been a blessing to me and an inspiration to want to pursue another level.

Acknowledgments

I'D LIKE TO thank:

My Lord and Savior Jesus Christ: for leading my life and allowing me to go to another level. Through Your love and grace You will allow me to one day see things eyes have not seen nor ears have heard.

My friend, love, and wife, Karen: for the sacrifices you have made and the patience you endured so I may bring forth something great.

My parents, Ellis and Eleanor Powell: thanks for encouraging me to be the best me I can be. I am an original.

My other parents (in-laws) Howard and Mary Robinson: thanks for always allowing me to be me.

My loving sister, Antoinette: thanks for supporting your big brother. It is always good to know you are back there.

To my church family (The Daily Bread, Inc.): you have been the edge to my game. You make me bring my best every time to the court. Thanks.

To my family, friends, and prayer partners in the ministry: thanks for all your support and belief. To the rest of my family: love, respect, and support one another, and we will all get there.

Special thanks:

My ravens, Arthur Johnson II and Dawn Sloan, who continued to remind me that I am closer than I really am. God has not forgotten. Let's do it then!

My great publishing team that God had selected at Creation House. Let this be the book that takes us all to the next level.

To all the many people whom I have met directly and indirectly and who might have been able to be a pair of jumper cables—to share words of strength, clarity, confidence, warmth, and comfort. I say thank you for allowing me to be a raven in your life. For it is you who have been my biggest fans as well the best team players. That has motivated and inspired me to labor even more because you appreciated what I had to offer.

To the people who read this book: this is my message to you. The world is waiting for you. It will make room for you. You know it is funny because the world loves to discover things that already existed. That treasure is you! You have been here the whole time; now it is your time. As you begin this journey things will become a lot clearer. So get ready as we start going to the next level!

CONTENTS

Introduction

WHAT ABOUT MY life? That is the question we all ask ourselves. Is life all about working, paying bills, family, and the daily hustle and bustle? We all seek to find the science and ultimate plan or purpose for our lives. I realize I am not an accident, and the earth, moon, sun, and other things were here long before I showed up. The question is what am I supposed to be doing while I am here? How do I contribute to society? God created everything and gave everything a gift inside to sustain its existence and allow everything to grow. Realizing this, God instructed Adam and Eve from the beginning to be fruitful and multiply.

Self-help books often suggest that you try to discover the meaning and purpose of your life by looking within yourself, but that is only partially the truth and is the secondary place to start. You must begin with God, your Creator, and

His reasons for creating you. You were made by God, and for God, and until you understand that, life will never make sense, and you will never be able to go to the next level.

The reason looking inside is secondary is because God has placed the hidden treasure inside of you. Just like a hidden treasure, the only way to find it is to either find the person who buried it or find the map that has the directions to the location. And if you think about the map, the only person that could have drawn the map is the very same person who buried the treasure. That person is God Himself. This book will help you understand that you need to seek out God first and develop a relationship with Him. For through this journey as you seek God out He will seek you out by revealing Himself to you more and more. It is through this amazing race that you will receive your prize.

Yes, there is a prize. The prize is the treasure chest that God has placed in your heart. Your chest is filled with all sorts of great gifts God has placed inside of you—such things as talents, abilities, skills, and desires which will allow you to have the abundant life that God wants us all to have. But is He who directs your path step by step leading you to this great discovery? It is very important that each of us recognize His voice when He speaks because our success in life is contingent upon this. Without sensing His presence, power, and spirit we will not go to the next level.

Believe it or not, God has spoken to each of us at some point in our lives. He used other people, situations, or signs to speak to us. This book will help you understand God is a good God because before we were born He gave us all some great gifts and put them in a treasure chest and buried them in us. God wants us to operate within His timing and plan.

I believe that during certain times of the year (seasons) some things are revealed on earth to help us find them a lot easier. As we allow God to lead us through this maze called life, it will reduce our stress, focus our energy, simplify our decisions, give meaning to life, and, importantly, giving us what we need to go to the next level.

Going to the next level is a blueprint to reach the maximum potential for anyone who follows the instructions of the treasure map laid out inside. This is a book of hope and challenge that you will read and re-read, and it will be true treasure for generations to come. Why? For all will see God in a different, clearer picture.

As you come to realize what you have and immediately start to put those treasures to work for you, please think about this: the only way you can open up a chest is by having the key. Understand that God is the Key and the Ultimate Treasure, which is also placed in you. This book will take you through a spiritual but practical journey that will challenge you and cause you to go higher while seeking God. This exploration will also transform your mind, heart, and spirit, and ultimately your life. Have fun going to the next level.

You don't have to be great to start, but you do have to start to be great.

—UNKNOWN

A man who does many things makes many mistakes, but he obviously doesn't make the biggest mistake of them all by doing nothing!

—UNKNOWN

The number of people who are unemployed isn't as great as the number of people who aren't working.

—FRANK CLARK

Now faith is the substance of things hoped for, the evidence of things not seen.

—HEBREWS 11:1, NKJV

A man's heart plans his way, but the LORD directs his steps.

—PROVERBS 16:9, NKJV

One

THE FIRST STEP

MAN WAS CREATED to rule and have dominion. Every male and female has that quality to rule, govern, conquer, triumph, and become victorious. That is an instinct that man has. Achieving is a God-given characteristic that God has passed on to His Creation. The Bible states when God finished His work in six days, He saw everything that He had made, and indeed, it was very good (Gen. 1:31).

Before we go any further, read the following thought and quote:

> Thought: "You change a man's mind, you change his life."

> Quote: "If you kneel before one, you can stand before many."

God had set out to conquer His goal, and He achieved it; it was pleasing to Him. When we set goals in our lives and work hard at them, what a joy it is. Think of a baby taking its first step. There is something that goes off inside, letting the baby know it has completed its goal. The time Mom baked her first cake and it came out just right. The first shelf Dad put together—and it's still standing. Those are goals that we have all achieved in life; goals that bring a joy that connects with man. I know everyone would like to experience the joy of going to that next level.

Where is my next level? We must all understand that we are all on different levels. That is why they have kindergarten, first grade, sixth grade, eighth grade, twelfth grade, college, and then postgraduate studies. You never stop going to the next level with God. God is a God of promotion. God is a God of evaluation. God is a God of building. God is a God of testing. You can't go to the next level without passing a test. In order for you to go to the next level, you must look forward to your test.

> Observe your thoughts, for they become your words! Your thoughts are the seeds that you plant in your mind, which is the soil.

When you were younger, you attended grade school, and at the end of the year you knew that it was a test time. After test time, there came summer break, and then you moved over into that next realm and that next level. Understand throughout Scriptures all of the apostles state to rejoice in times of testing, trials, and tribulations. You might be asking,

"Why? Why would I ever rejoice in a time of hard times, struggling and difficulties?" The apostles understood that without a test one could not be promoted.

Note: Observe your thoughts, for they become your words! Your thoughts are the seeds that you plant in your mind, which is the soil. Look at this illustration: If a farmer plants apple seeds, he gets back apple trees. If he plants carrots, he gets back carrots. Of course, the same is true if a man plants fear and worries. He will reap more fear and worries. What allows both to grow is one's faith or belief. Your faith is the water that continues to feed and allow those seeds to stay alive and bring forth fruit. Are you allowing your faith to grow things you should not have planted? Don't panic! Just like a farmer, all you have to do is get on your knees and pull those things up. Pluck up all those bad thoughts and toss them away.

During your planting process, no matter what, it never fails that your soil will produce some weeds. Those weeds, if you don't work hard and pull them up, will become strongholds in your life and hinder you from reaching your goals. The weeds are at times your doubts and people that, if you are not careful, will choke the life out of your goals and dreams. These things serve no value at all, but they are what one must deal with on his way to going to the next level. Scripture states that if you don't watch it, these wild vines will pull all you have worked for down. (Read the parable of the sower in Matthew 13:1–10.) If you understand gardening, you know that the only way weeds cover your flowerbed is if you neglect to tend to it. You must continue to monitor your thoughts of doubt and do not let them fester, or they will become deeply rooted.

Remember, one of the keys to going to the next level is time. Nothing happens overnight, and that includes your success in life. If you fail to watch for those weeds, they will develop strong roots and require a lot more work to pull them up. Sometimes throughout our lives, we pull the weeds up from the surface, and yet, they still exist because we did not deal with the root of the problem. Without understanding what you are facing, you cannot triumph over it. God wants you to identify your opposition so you may conquer it. It is your opposition, your enemy, who keeps you from becoming the champion you are called to be. Keep in mind that your opposition is a worthy opponent; it knows your weakness and your strengths. It has studied your habits for years and knows how you think. But thank God for it, because on the other side of your opposition is the next level.

Nothing happens overnight, and that includes your success in life.

Your fears have built up a wall that you must penetrate. It stands and keeps you away from the rewards, benefits, dreams, goals, and destiny. Believe me, the only way you can defeat it is by the four *p's* of purpose, which we will talk about later in this book. The challenge you are faced with is part of your test that God wants you to pass so He can get you going to the next level. All that you need God has already equipped you with. Now that's good news! God wants to train you, so develop those muscles He gave to you! Your opposition is what will bring those out in you. People go through life repeating life lessons over and over simply because they have not passed their test yet. I call this the "merry-go-round syndrome." You continue to go around and around until you pass the test and get off this ride.

I'm sure life has shown you some things over and over, and you reacted like I have: "Haven't I seen this before?" The answer is yes. God is giving you another chance to pass the test, and if you continue to make the wrong choice, you will have to wait until the next season to take the test again. The moment you pass it, your life changes and you are on your way to the next level. This will require prayer, discipline, commitment, and time. You can walk a thousand miles, but it starts with the first step! Let's refer to a familiar story regarding the prophet Elijah in 1 Kings 17.

> And Elijah the Tishbite, of the inhabitants of Gilead...
> —1 Kings 17:1

Elijah was a prophet of God. One would say he was the greatest prophet in the Old Testament, yet we see here clearly that by him being one of the greatest prophets in the Old Testament, he clearly had a relationship with God.

If you are getting ready to go to the next level, the first thing you must do is have a relationship with God. He is the Teacher. He is the Creator. How can you possibly get promoted to next grade level when you don't have the relationship and the connection with the teacher? Jesus said, "It is expedient that I go back to My Father, but I will send you one back like Me. I will send you the Holy Spirit *who will guide you and teach you.*" (See John 16.) We must have a relationship with the Teacher. We must have a relationship with the Master. We must have a relationship with the Father.

That is the first thing we must do. Parents, if you hear

that your kids are struggling and having a communication problem or misunderstanding with the teacher, I suggest you get to the school quick. If you don't, your child will soon fail. You'll say, "What happened, Jimmy?," and he'll reply, "I just couldn't make the connection and have the relationship with the teacher." Have you ever noticed too that when they're struggling in a relationship with the teacher, they say, "Maybe she just doesn't like me. She's just picking on me." No, the real problem is you're struggling to make that connection. That is why you are having a hard time with that simple subject she's teaching you.

As human beings we all need to make that spiritual connection and have a relationship with God. He is a God of promotion. Understand that when God created the earth He gave man dominion over it. But man has to be trained. If we do not establish a relationship with God, we will struggle in life and feel as if God (the teacher) has forsaken us. Without it man is left teaching himself about himself. Of course, we know from His Word that He will never leave us or forsake us (Heb. 13:5).

We must make time with God so He may teach us to have a daily relationship with Him. Life is the course that we all must take. Life is full of pop quizzes daily. Jesus said, "I have overcome the world" (John 16:33). Jesus aced the course, and all who desire to pass need His guidance. Jesus clearly states here that He has all the answers to life's questions: "I am the way, the truth, and the life. No one comes to the Father except through Me" (John 14:6). We struggle through life because we lack the knowledge of God, and since we don't have the answers throughout life we panic. God wrote the test, and since the fall of man (Adam) no man has passed; all have failed and fallen short of the glory of God (Rom. 3:23). Jesus came prepared from heaven, and He studied for the test. Not only did He pass life's test, but also He made the perfect score. Jesus stated He is the truth. This means that His life, power, and ministry are the answer. Jesus' life is an open book for all to read, to study, and to model so that they may be equipped to pass life's test. Jesus also stated that He is the way. He stated that any man who follows Him and disciplines himself will reach his goal and go to the next level. I know you are as excited as I am about going to the next level, so let's take another step.

> And Elijah the Tishbite, of the inhabitants of Gilead, said to Ahab…
>
> —1 KINGS 17:1

Ahab was an evil and wicked king.

> Now Ahab the son of Omri did evil in the sight of the LORD, more than all who were before him.
>
> —1 KING 16:31

Ahab was a bad individual and represented a bad situation. I have had some bad times, and I am sure you can relate. Things went wrong, rather it be the car, washer/dryer, job, marriage, kids, health, or finances. Ahab had built wooden images of Baal and worshiped them. The worship of Baal was a representation of anything and everything except for God. When you start to worship anything more than God, you're getting to be like Ahab. That is evil in the sight of God. You start to praise and worship money, material things, and people. You're becoming like Ahab. The Scripture says Ahab provoked

God more than anybody. Perhaps this was a result of his being so evil, provoking God to do some things that He wasn't going to do.

Have you ever been provoked? You might say something like, "Don't make me do this." "All right now, you keep pushing it." That was Ahab. At the same point and time, Ahab was evil and wicked. This kind of reminds you of the god of this world we have here, called Satan, doesn't it? He does more evil and wicked things than anybody you can imagine. He has been that way from the beginning; he'll be that way to the end. When those things come up in your life that seem to want to tear your marriage down, your finances down, your body down, your mind down—those are the AHABS. Those are things that are coming into your life that are not pleasing to God. We are going to be like Elijah and learn from him.

> And Elijah the Tishbite, of the inhabitants of Gilead, said to Ahab. "As the LORD God of Israel lives, before whom I stand, there shall not be dew nor rain these years, except at my word."
> —1 KINGS 17:1

You must stand up and tell those Ahabs in your life, "Sure as my God lives, this isn't going to happen." Sure you're going to have people come up in your life and tell you, "What are you going to do now?" You answer them, "Sure as my God lives, this isn't going to happen." Isaiah 54:17 tells us that no weapon formed against us shall prosper. I don't care if the factory at work is closing down. I don't care if my company is laying people off. I don't care if gas prices are going up. I don't care if all of this is happening in this world. It doesn't have anything to do with me. You have to stand up boldly to those evil and wicked things that are popping up in your life and say, "I won't stand for it." That is what Elijah said, "I won't stand for it."

The first thing we must do is *speak those things*. Scriptures states there is life and death in the power of the tongue (Prov. 18:21). There are blessings and curses in the tongue. What are you speaking? When life poses you the difficult questions, are you going to the Teacher who has all answers? Or are you being overwhelmed and overburdened by its impact because you are trying to do it by yourself? Remember the old nursery rhyme about Humpty Dumpty?

> Humpty Dumpty sat on the wall,
> Humpty Dumpty had a great fall,
> All the king's horses
> And all the king's men,
> Couldn't put Humpty back together again.

Why? Because no one asked the King? God said, "Let there be light," and there was light (Gen. 1:3). His Word, which is Jesus, created all creation. God believed in His Word because His Word has all power. Scripture states that even God calls those things that do not exist as though they did. Do you have faith and hope in your Word? Notice I said in your *Word* and not your *words*. In order for you to obtain what you are saying, you must have confidence in whom you are claiming. You see, what you say becomes your actions.

If I may use an illustration here, just because a person says every day he will be a millionaire doesn't mean that he or she will be. That person must believe in what he or she is saying. If not, it won't happen. On the other hand, if you have a person who speaks that one day he or she will be a millionaire and believes just that, then his or her actions will reflect just that. Illustration: Only a farmer who believes one day that he will have a harvest will start to sow seeds. Your actions today are seeds planted for tomorrow's harvest. Your actions are what chisel, form, and frame your future. Your words and actions work as a team.

I am sure Ahab walked around, trying to implant and impart fear on Elijah. Elijah stood up and said, "Hold up now. You are not the master of it all. You don't have all power." If I have God, I fear no situation. No weapon formed against me shall prosper, nor shall any enemy conquer me! Fear no man and fear none of your circumstances, because that's just what they are. I'm not scared of folks running around here bombing and doing all of these missions of suicide attacks. My God is my protector. My God is my provider. He is my source. But God is looking for people to stand up in faith.

The second thing you must do is *stand up*. When was the last time you stood up and said, "I'm not taking this anymore because surely my God lives and reigns forever and ever"? He has all power of heaven and earth. I fear no man. If you want to lose weight, then you tell that body, "I'm standing up today. You're getting in check and in shape." I'm sure the body is going to say, "Say what?" No, today this is it.

Your actions today are seeds planted for tomorrow's harvest.

Today is the day I'm standing up. All of those foolish and wicked thoughts that come in your mind will start to say,

"Well, you know I can't have this…well, you know I can't do this…well, you know I can't be this." Stand up! When are you going to stand up? That is the question.

In the Book of Acts there was a lame man who was sitting at the edge of the gate when the disciples walked by. He was sitting there, begging for money. He was asking for some silver or gold. They told him, "Silver and gold I do not have, but what I do have I give you" (Acts 3:6). In other words, "I'm going to give you a Word. Stand up! Take up your mat and go home." In order for you to move to the next level you must stand up and make the next step. The apostle James wrote, "Draw near to God and He will draw near to you" (James 4:8).

Third, when the Word of God comes to you, you have to be willing to receive it, believe it, and *stand on it.* Stand on it! That is what Elijah did. He stood on God's Word. God's Word is the rock. Jesus stated that a man is wise if he builds his house on rock. If any man stands on the rock, no matter how bad the waves tend to toss to and fro, it will not move him! When is the last time you stood up and stood on His Word? Elijah said that it's not going to rain. It's not going to drop one drop in three years. He stood on God's Word. Scripture states that God is not a man, so He cannot lie (Num. 23:19). It also states that God does not change and is the same yesterday, today, and forever more (Heb. 13:8). It is He who is able to keep you from falling, and it is He who is able to keep you from failing. Scripture states that His Word holds everything together (Heb. 1:3). God will hold your goals, desires, and life together so that you trust Him.

Lastly, once you speak God's Word, stand up to your

situation or mountain, and stand on His Rock, then you want to *stand back!* This one is a tough one for us all. For Scripture states, "'For My thoughts are not your thoughts, nor are your ways My ways,' says the LORD" (Isa. 55:8). God has His own way of doing things. It is like having a dispute with someone and you call the policeman. Once he gets there, you have to give up all authority while he assumes it. He is now handling the situation. Once one of higher authority has assumed responsibility, you have to submit. God said it, and then watch what's going to happen. If God said you could have that promotion, then watch what's going to happen. If God said you're getting ready to move to that next level, then watch Him! But you have to stand up and stand on; otherwise, you will be moved.

We're getting ready to go to the next level. As the Lord God of Israel lives and for whom I stand, if I stand in agreement with God, then surely these things must happen. If I'm connected and have a relationship with the teacher, the As and Bs must come. Am I making it plain? All I have to do is stand in agreement with the teacher, and the rest will take care of itself. Scripture states, "Can two walk together, unless they are agreed?" (Amos 3:3). So for all of those evil things that Ahab tried to bring about, Elijah says, "No, I'm going to stand on God's Word, and whatever God says, then that is it. And I'll wait and stand on it."

Throughout all the miracles of the Bible, you will notice there was one thing and one theme stated. One would say, "I know what that was. That was the need." Well, yes there was a need. There is always a need. When it came to the money situation, that was what Judas was talking about: "The money, we could have given it to the poor." And Jesus said the poor will always be among you (Matt. 26:11). That pretty much says there is always going to be a need. People say, "Well, it's going to take faith and belief." Well, yes and no. There are a lot of people in scripture who didn't know God and still got a miracle. So, that can't be the common theme. The common theme is having a problem. Do you have a problem that needs to be worked out? If you have a problem, that itself makes you a candidate for a miracle. Jesus is a miracle worker. He is a problem solver. I have had many that I have handed over to Him; I saw those things come to pass. He says if you stand up and stand on, then stand back and get ready. Look out and get ready to go to the next level.

Then the word of the LORD came to him.

—1 KINGS 17:2

When? Then. When? Right now. The minute he said it and stood up, stood on, and stood back—Bam! When he did those three things, then the Lord showed up. Everything is condition. If you do this, He'll do that. If you don't do this, don't expect Him to do that. As you can see, He keeps His word. The scripture says, "Then." That means something had to happen before.

Then the Lord. Then the word of the Lord came to him. See, God goes through the valleys, searching and seeking for people who are willing to speak His Word to those Ahabs…to speak to their current situations and say, "I'm standing up." "I'm not taking this anymore from you." "You're not picking on me anymore." "You're not taking my lunch money anymore." "You're not taking my joy anymore." "You're not taking all of the great things God has done for me." It tries to get you distracted and lose focus. It is like being in grade school and you have people saying, "*Psst, psst.*" You say, "Be quiet, I'm trying to focus on what the teacher is teaching. To get my word. To get my lesson. To get my blessing for my life." But what are the Ahabs going to do? "*Psst, psst.*" But you say to them, "Hey. I'm not talking to you. You're trying to take away what I'm trying to get." Because the Ahabs know that if you listen and get this, then you're bound to go to the next level.

> Then the word of the LORD came to him, saying, Get away from here and turn eastward.
>
> —1 KINGS 17:2

Get away from here. God says "Hear me! The enemy knows, because he has peeked into your future, that you're about to go to the next level. So what you have to do is get out of here." God says, "Get away from this crowd! Get out of this atmosphere and get to a place I have for you. I have to pull you up from all these weeds. If you stay in a bad situation for so long, it distorts you. It takes away what's in you." God says, "You have to get out of this. Those individuals you've been running around with, those folks you socializing with at work, you can't do that anymore. They are called Distracters, because they are not going in the direction I'm taking you. They are distracting you and leading you off course, and in time it will lead to a disaster."

Illustration: It's like someone who has planned a trip, and he is at the airport. While waiting for his flight he runs into some old friends or even family members, and they begin to talk. Through the conversation they realize their flights are at the same time and with the same airline, but at different terminals and to different destinations. All too well we miss our flight that would carry us to the destiny God has prepared for us at a certain time, or we catch the wrong flight carrying us further away from our destiny. Beware of distracters! If not, you will sooner or later find yourself going in the opposite direction. Travel with people who will play a part in making sure you make your flight on time.

Can two walk together, unless they are agreed?
—Amos 3:3

You have to surround yourself with people who are walking in the same direction as you are, or at least have been where you are trying to go! God will send angels who will encourage you, help you, and even support you all the way. These people I refer to as "angels" or "partners" because they will be filled with the love of God. Your partners will take the time to invest in you. They cherish the idea that when you make it, they made it, too. The individuals have sacrificed their time, money, family, and life to assure that their stock, which is you, rise to the top. Or God will send you a mentor or coach that you will have favor with. The coaches are there to help you develop and enhance the gift that God deposited inside of you along your journey. They too have invested in you, but just like a "certificate of deposit"—CD, they realize it takes time before it matures. I will discuss this more in the next chapter. But, you have to be sensitive to the Spirit and listening to what He tells you. Get away from the distracters! They are not going your way.

But then you have the stubborn ones, and they will go along anyway. And then they wonder why they are so far away from their destiny. Your destiny is X, waiting on you. And you're all the way to Y. Most of us have arrived at Y—why? *Why am I here? Where did I go wrong?* God has predestined our trip, from the departure all the way to the arrival. I referred to your destiny as X earlier. X marks the spot. God buried His treasure for you at X. He has deliberately put the code in His Word. The Bible is His map, and as you develop a relationship with Him, He will guide your path.

Here is the beautiful thing about God. Not only does He tell you what you need, but He also tells you where to go get it. He says, "Get away from here and turn eastward." Is He not a God of direction? You say, "I'll get away, Lord, but where am I going to go?" He says, "Child, turn here and go there."

There are times in our life when we follow those instructions and listen and say, "This is a word from God, and I am not moving. I know He told me to do this! I know He told me to work on this and work on that and become this and become that. OK, so I'm here, so what do I do?" He says, "Turn here." So I turn here. When we turn, we say, "Hey, there's no one here!"

Sometime you will have to walk alone. Are you willing to do that? Are you willing to walk alone at times, knowing this is the direction that God sent you in? In order to get to the next level, you must be willing to follow instructions and move past your fear. "For God has not given us a spirit of fear, but of power and of love and of a sound mind" (2 Tim. 1:7).

So Elijah turned eastward, and there was nobody there. But I want you to take this and be sure that if you're following His directions, you are allowing Him to guide your path. That is what a righteous man does. But see, there is nobody here. Sometimes God has to get you off by yourself to see if you are willing to endure the tough times. Are you willing to gut it out? Or, when the going gets tough, do you get going? Understand this: if you know deep in your heart whatever it may be that God said to do, that settles the matter, because it is already blessed. It has the happiness, joy, and riches connected to it.

Your gift will unlock it. Stop trying to convince other people of what God has planned for you. Remember He told *you*, not the world! Do not take your focus off of it. Every day you get up in the morning and tell yourself, "I am on the right flight, and I am on time for my destiny." Let God be the tower that controls your plane (spirit), Jesus be the pilot that controls your mind, and the Holy Spirit be the copilot that controls your heart—and you control your actions/works by following the instructions of the cabinet. If not, you will lose faith and heart, and your plane will start to descend and fall well short of its destination. If you are going to get to the next level, you must be willing to ignore some things and some people. You have to be willing to sow the labor to reap the reward.

> Get away from here and turn eastward, and hide by the Brook Cherith.
>
> —1 KINGS 17:3

Hide. Jesus walked among the crowds many times. But He always took time. Then the very next scripture states He just disappeared. He got away to focus on God. If you want

21

to get to your destiny, you have to sometimes just hide your-self away from people. People will say "I haven't seen you in a while." You can say, "I needed some quiet time." Be straight up with people. "I've been hiding because I need a word. I need a sense of direction. I need a purpose. I couldn't get it hanging around everybody. I'm hearing too many voices. I need to hear one, and He speaks soft but clear. I can't hear around everyone else because it is distracting and confus-ing. I needed clarity and confirmation."

Have you ever noticed when you hide things, you only hide things that are important to you? Sometimes you hide something so well, you forget where you put it. But that is just to show you how important that thing is to you. That is what God does to us. He loves us so much that He is willing to hide us from the world. He says, "No one will get to you because you are valuable to me. So, I'm going to hide him. I'm going to restore her. I'm going to build him up and then put him back out there."

Some of us are being restored. Some of us are being built back up. So He is hiding us. When one is being hidden, one is protected. When you also hide something, you hide it to protect it. He hides us. He protects us from all of those Ahabs. Those evil and wicked situations that come within our life. Being broke. Being hurt. Distressed. Despair and whatever conditions you feel you have been bound and bur-dened with. Those are wicked and evil things. Things that a child of God should not endure. So He says, "Follow My instructions. Stand up to it, and when you do that, I will speak to you, tell you where to go, and then I'll hide you. I'm getting you ready to go to the next level."

Hide by the Brook Cherith, which flows into the
Jordan. And it will be that you shall drink from the
brook, and I have commanded the ravens to feed you
there.

—1 KINGS 17:3–4

Elijah had stood up against the situation that came
against him. So when God told him to leave, turn eastward,
there was no water and no food. In the Old Testament
times, if you had no water and no food, you would soon die,
because you lived off the land. That was a source of survival.
We have those things now. They're called God, family, jobs,
money, health, sound mind, and peace.

But He says, "When you follow my instructions and get
to the brook, then you can drink water there." So we must
have faith and go. Believe that God's Word is true. Scripture states that God is not a man; therefore, He cannot lie.
(See Numbers 23:19.) There will be times when we all will
have to go alone to reach our destiny. Just know this—the
brook is on the other side. Know that the only thing that
keeps you from it is you giving up. Trust me; if you have
reached this far, you will continue to have that thirst for the
brook. The what if? The regret? The doubt? The misfortune?
Again I believe truly all the fulfillment and riches are tied
to the brook. He says "When you get there, it'll be there.
It'll be there."

But your concern is, "What am I going to do about
my job? My marriage? My kids? What am I going to do
about this? What am I going to do about that?" He says,
"Don't worry about that. Since you stood up (to your situation), stood on (My Word), and are now standing back
(being patient and waiting on My perfect timing), things

will unfold before your eyes because you have followed My instructions. When you get to this place that I have for you, it'll be there. Drink however much you want. The river flows. This is not a pond. It flows. You cannot stop it. All that you used to lack, you have plenty of it now. It just keeps flowing in your life, when you're following instructions." When you're getting ready to go to the next level, the Bible states, "Draw near to God and He will draw near to you" (James 4:8).

It's your move! Make the first step!

Coming together is a beginning, staying together is process, and working together is success.

—Henry Ford

We're all one idea or one person away from everything we could ever want.

—Ellis Powell

Then he sent out a raven, which kept going to and fro until the waters had dried up from the earth.

—Genesis 8:7, nkjv

He sent His word and healed them, and delivered them from their destructions.

—Psalms 107:20, nkjv

Let brotherly love continue. Do not forget to entertain strangers, for by so doing some have unwittingly entertained angels.

—Hebrews 13:1–2, nkjv

Two

THE RAVENS ARE COMING

LOOK AT 1 Kings 17:4:

And I have commanded the ravens to feed you there.

"I have ordered the ravens to feed you." Keep in mind that the distracters will be there. I am sure you have heard all of the following phrases: "I don't know why you're going over there, they're not hiring." You have to stand on God's Word: "God told me they are hiring, so somehow, some way they are going to hire me." "I don't know why you working so hard, there is a hiring freeze. They are not promoting anybody." "I'm going to get promoted." If God said it, that settles it. No matter what you do, you work for God. He will acknowledge you. He will always send that person/angel/raven in your life to bless you. Case in point: Have you ever asked God for something—a job, promotion, house, loan, car, etc.? And did you hear this infamous phrase: "We don't normally do this, but in your case we will"? I believe those people were sent in your path to bless you, to feed you at your point of need. Just like Elijah.

Another example: "You know, I went to HR, and there really was no position open, but something told them to create one." That's a raven, again. As you can see, God has been sending ravens all through your life, and the exciting thing is He has more to send out on your behalf. Scripture states:

> For it is written: "He shall give His angels charge over you, to keep you."

God has put people in your life to protect you and make sure you succeed. But all of those Ahabs will say, "No, it's not going to happen for you, I don't see it." That's why you have to get yourself away from them. They can't see what He has for you. You have people call the grim reapers, who literally will talk your dream *to death*. The negativity and doubt will literally burst your bubble if you don't watch. Have you ever talked to an individual and the attitude and outlook was so pessimistic, that you started to wonder about your destiny? You felt like putting your flight on hold? Those are the grim reapers. They have spoken death for so long, all that listens, their dreams start to die slowly. Beware of these negative individuals.

God has put people in your life to protect you and make sure you succeed.

It's sad to say, but sometimes it's your family. King David experienced that from his own brother when he inquired about fighting Goliath. Goliath was part of his destiny, but his own brother tried to talk him out of it. His brother never realized that not only would it benefit David and himself, but also his whole entire family and the WHOLE nation of Israel.

Your own friends whom you thought were close to you will also abandon you, just as many disciples did to Jesus in His ministry. Some will end their relationship with you and start to either despise you or become jealous, just like the brothers of Joseph did when he told them about his dream. Know this: most folks become jealous because they view themselves as small. It's not so much that they do not want you to have your dream or destiny, but they cannot ever see themselves with theirs. Therefore, you should not have yours either. They never consider the faith and work it took to get it. The "breaks," as one would call it, are part of the path. Scripture states that God is no respecter of persons (Acts 10:34); therefore, He shows no favoritism or partiality. What is done for one will be done for all. That includes you, too.

I've wondered why God would pick the ravens. Ravens are scavengers. They survive by looking for food. They will fly miles and miles looking for carcasses as food. God didn't tell Elijah buzzards would feed him. He didn't say vultures would feed him. He said ravens. He selected a particular bird. He selects a particular person or guardian angel who will look after you. These particular birds will fly miles and miles looking for food. There are people who will do whatever it takes to get it done. God said, "I'm going to put you with those people. I'm going to put you with people who are going to help you reach your destination and who are willing to do whatever it takes to get you there. I'm going to put you with those folks who are willing to stay up all night and get up early to get there."

Ravens! Ravens! They are willing to do whatever it takes to make sure you survive. He says, "I'm going to put you with them because they will make sure that your dreams come to pass." Don't put me with just anybody. Put me with some ravens. People who will make sure you stay focused and on point. They will hold you accountable and will encourage you when you are feeling low. They will address you with the following phrases: "How is your day going?" "Are you working on your goals?" "How are you doing?" Those are ravens. "Anything I can do to help you?" "Anything you need?" Those are ravens. You say, "No, I'm fine, but that food of confidence and encouragement sure helped me. It sure fed my spirit, just when I was about to quit and give up."

But then here comes a raven, with a word from God. "Are you almost through yet with your goals?" "How are you coming along?" You're saying to yourself, "Lord, actually, I thought You had forgotten all about me." But He sent a raven into your life to bring you that bread on time. Isn't He good? "I'll send the ravens to you, to feed you."

Surely, they were not there when Elijah got to the brook. I'm sure he was looking for them. "Where are they?" So he went and did according to the word of the Lord. There was another step. It didn't say he saw. So he went based on the word of God. Scripture states that man shall not live by bread alone, but by every word that proceeded out of the mouth of God (Matt. 4:4).

Once Elijah got his word from God, the scripture says, "And he went." He hasn't seen anything yet. But if God said it, I'm on my way. Some folks are carnal. Superficial. They have to see things first. But, if God said it. Well.

Have you gone yet? Or are you still there? Are you still in the same situation that you were before? In the first chapter we learned that you must make the first step in order to have something that you've never had. You must be willing to do something that you've never done.

Elijah had never been to brook Cherith. Where is that? God said, "Don't worry about that. You just go." So we have to go to the place God has ordained for us because that is our true destiny. So he went and did according to the word of the Lord. All of those are steps. Any one of those things that you miss out on means you haven't fulfilled the word. You have not truly followed the instructions.

> In order to have something that you've never had, you must be willing to do something that you've never done.

Illustration: Anyone who does not bake from scratch uses cake mix. Well, there are instructions on the box. Step 1, step 2, steps 3, 4, 5, and so forth. If you follow those steps, your cake will look like the cake on the box. If you miss any of these steps, there is *no guarantee* from the maker that the cake will look like the cake on the box. You must follow the given instructions. For the instructions are already blessed and will manifest what it said it would. You must do according to what He said.

Well, I don't know if I should go here. OK, you're changing the whole design. You're changing the entire mixture now. Don't expect your cake to look like this…nor your life. You've changed it. You failed to believe the Creator. But we learned that Elijah went to the brook—the place God had anointed for him—and did according to the word of the Lord. There's a place God has already blessed for you. All you have to do is get there. Most folks get there and leave. Did you ever get to a place for an event someone has invited you to, and you arrive maybe a bit early, and say to yourself, "Maybe this isn't the place," and you just pull off? Then they call you later and say, "Where are you?" You reply, "I was just there, but I didn't stay, because I didn't see anything."

You didn't stay. That is another step. Be patient and wait. Trust in Him. If He sent you there, it'll be there. Stay there. This is your anointed place. The ravens hadn't showed up yet. If you leave, you miss out on the raven God is sending to you. Scripture tells us that God does everything with perfect timing, with decency, and in order. I'm trying to get you to go to the next level. God has used this man's situation. Evil and tough times have come up on him. He stood up on it, and God said, "I'm going to use that to get the glory and the praise out of it."

God used a bad situation. If you are dealing with a bad situation or need God to bring your dream to reality or simply believe God for the impossible, step right up. That puts you in the line to go to the next level. See, when you stand up to your situation, whether it be turmoil at work, turmoil at home, in your family relationship, in your finances, in your mind, then God is able to do something for you. But you have to stand up. You cannot let this wicked and evil thing bully you in your life. If it is something you want, then you have to get to the point that you say, "I'm going to stand up to this giant." David had to do the same thing when it came to Goliath.

But before he stood up to it, he inquired on what the

31

rewards would be for knocking this giant down.

What are the other rewards if I stand up to my bad finances? One is good credit, two is having some money in the bank. Three is alleviating those troubled and stressful times. What are the rewards if I stand up and fight for my marriage? One is peace in my home. Two is love that I had lost. I can have that love back. I can set a good example for my children and my family to show them a godly model and relationship.

There is nothing but rewards. But you have to stand up to your giant. That is what we're talking about. That is what you have to do to get yourself ready to go to the next level. People say, "I'm ready to go to the next level. I'm ready. I'm ready." But have you stood up yet? If you haven't stood up, then you're not ready. When you stand up, then you know that you're not alone. David said, "I have been young, and now am old; yet I have not seen the righteous forsaken, nor his descendants begging bread" (Ps. 37:25). You're not by yourself anymore. But you have to call on Him. He needs something to work with.

We've all been to school growing up, and you have this bully in school. It seems the bully never has anything better to do than seek and find you. You're like, "Oh, here he comes." But today is going to have to be the day that you stand up into whatever you're lacking and hurting in your situation. I had to deal with the same bully. When I got home, I told my dad about it. I said "Hey, this bully is bothering me at school."

My daddy said, "I hear you." The first thing he asked me, which simply lines up with the Bible, was "Did you stand up to him?"

I replied "Well, no."

And my dad said, "Well don't come talking to me until you've stood up to him. Let me see what you've got. How about you let me see and let yourself see what you've really got inside of you. Have you stood up?"

I said "But if I stand up, this bully is likely to knock me out!"

My dad said, "I'm behind you." When I heard "I am behind you," I couldn't wait until the next day! As a matter of fact, I went back looking for the bully. I'm all right now, because my raven had fed me encouraging words and I was no longer afraid. But I had to stand up first. Whatever you're fighting for and asking God for in your life, you have to stand up! Then stand on and believe His promise to know that He has you.

> For he [Elijah] went and stayed by the Brook Cherith, which flows into the Jordan.
>
> —1 Kings 17:5

Now notice that when he went there, he stayed. A lot of times, we get to the place that God has for us and get impatient. We don't want to wait. Well, that comes with refining and bringing out the character within you. God says, "I am trying to bring something out of you. Patience is a virtue. Patience is a must." Even today, the microwave takes a few moments. You can rush it however you want to. But nothing is quite instant. We know that God created everything in six days. Why did He do it in six days? Couldn't He just have snapped his finger? Yes, He could've done that, but in essence, everything is done in seasons, in time.

When you stand up, you simply tell the world, "It is my

time!" It is your time. Now, the ravens have not come yet. So you must stay there until the ravens come. In 1 Kings 17:4 the Lord says, "I have commanded the ravens to feed you there." I've ordered them to feed you. Of all the birds out there, why the raven? You never hear about the raven. You hear about how the Holy Spirit falls upon you, like a dove. You hear about "Mount up with wings like eagles" (Isa. 40:31). A raven? Why would God send a raven? We're going to talk about that. That's what we're going to focus on, because that is what's getting you ready to go to the next level. While we stand there and wait, what kind of bird should we be waiting on? A raven. So that means there is a particular bird God has for you, not just any bird. There is a particular bird.

The ravens are coming! The ravens are coming! That is the next sign to your next level. Know that God has you in the right place. You say, "I'm here now; where are my ravens?" Well, you'll have to wait!

One thing we understand about ravens is that they are all in a particular place. They do not go to far from their territory, but you have to wait for them to get there. "So I have the job. I have the house. I have the relationship. So where are these things? You say You're going to send me, Lord?" Again, that is another level that God is trying to take you to in order to perfect you, to work on you inside. We must understand that God has already chosen someone just for you. Make no mistake about it. This is not an accident. Nor will it be a coincidence. There is a saying that people use all the time: "We just bumped into each other today." Oh no! God says, "I had chosen this raven a long time ago. I was just waiting for you to stand up to your situation or dream.

Now I am going to send a particular bird for you."
Let's look at 1 Kings 17:6.

> The ravens brought him bread and meat in the morning, and bread and meat in the evening; and he drank from the brook.

The ravens will remind you that God is able…God is good. They will feed you and nourish you with phrases such as, "Let me tell you what God has done for me." "Anything I can do for you, just call me." That's feeding. That is meat. That is substance. The bread. Jesus said, "I am the bread of life" (John 6:48). Ravens will always speak a word of God into your life. That's what ravens do—speak words of encouragement and inspiration.

Are you a raven? Do you go around feeding people meat and bread? That's what it takes to go to the next level. Jesus has told us that when you do those things, you can expect those things in your life. If you want a friend, then show yourself friendly. If you want ravens to come, why don't you turn into a raven? When is the last time you just called and encouraged somebody? When is the last time you said, "Hey, I heard what you were going through. I heard you stood up against your Ahab. I hear you are working on your dream, and I just want to say, Go for it! I heard those things are going on in your life, but don't worry, because our God is able! He is more than the world against you, and through Him, you are more than a conqueror."

The ravens will remind you that God is able… God is good.

That is what a raven does. Example: When you got your first job and didn't have a clue about what to do, a raven flies over to you and says, "How are you doing? I know today is your first day, and I'm willing to show you whatever it takes to make your job and your life easier." All you can say in the secret corner of your heart is "Thank You, Lord. I didn't have a clue, but You sent a raven my way."

Example: Have you ever been lost and had no clue how to get to where you were going and someone gave you directions? You smiled and felt better. That was a raven!

My question to you is: Are you a raven? If not, let's talk about some other birds He could have sent and let's see if you're that bird. He could have sent a dove. We hear about doves quite often in Scripture. You must understand that whatever you're going through, God has someone specifically for that situation. Illustration—if I am trying to remove a bolt or a nut from something, I don't need a screwdriver. I need a crescent wrench or a pair of pliers. I have a specific need. A Phillips screwdriver won't do. I need something to take this off! When I get to a screw or something else, then I'll need that. This is the way God works: He knows our every need. He won't send something you don't need!

So why didn't God send a dove to Elijah? I went back and looked at a dove and learned about his character. You can look at the character of the people that God sends to you. A bird's call or cry is the bird's communication. The bird is letting you know what's inside of that bird. A dove is a variety of bird that includes the pigeon. A dove advocates peace and opposes conflict. That's why the Word says to be "harmless as doves" (Matt. 10:16). Don't a start mess and don't create a conflict. A dove is all about peace. When things are going wrong, a dove appears and says, "We shouldn't be doing all of that." When you hear about someone going through a bad situation…their marriage is in trouble…their finances are in trouble…their body is in trouble…their mind is in trouble…don't talk about that person when they are going through bad things. A dove is there for your comfort. Everything is going to be all right. Don't worry about those folks talking about you. You are going to be all right, sister or brother! That's what a dove does.

Are you that dove? Are you that dove, that no matter what goes on in the family, what goes on in your community, what goes on at the job, are you that one who simply brings peace when someone has suffered loss? Thank God for the dove. But in Elijah's situation, he didn't need a dove. He needed someone who was going to bring meat! A dove is not a big bird. It is a small bird, but it meets its need. Has God ever sent doves in your life, doves who have just simply said, "Hey, I just called to check on you"? They don't bring anymore than that, but just that brings comfort. God has sent many doves in my life during my stressful and tough times. I know sometimes the world can bring a lot of heat on you, and I want you to know that God is there for you. I'm all right after speaking to a dove.

Now a pigeon is part of the dove family, but a pigeon has a prominent chest and short legs. Prominence projects an outward appearance, and short legs don't stand tall. Has God ever sent you pigeons in your life? There are people who have their chests stuck out and say, "Look at me. Look at what I have," but they have short legs. They don't stand for a whole lot! It would have been nice if the pigeon had a raven mentality, because it has its chest stuck out for all its accomplishments. But a pigeon will not help you out. That's why a pigeon is not a raven. The first thing you will see in the dictionary is that a pigeon has a bulky chest—pride. Proud of what I've done. You have to be careful about a pigeon because they think they are better than everyone else.

You don't see a lot of pigeons together. You hear things about a lot of pigeons hanging together in the park. But they are there for eating. After they eat, they're gone. So God won't send you that. You don't need that right now. You need someone who can feed you meat and bread! You need encouragement, inspiration, for strenghening you because you just stood up. You need someone in your corner. Without someone in your corner, you are going to be defeated! We all know a pigeon. You went to school with a pigeon or worked with a pigeon. Some of us have pigeons in our family. They emulate that they're better. So that is why God didn't send Elijah a pigeon. A pigeon wouldn't do Elijah any good, because a pigeon is all about self.

What about an eagle? Why didn't God send an eagle? After all, an eagle is a large bird. An eagle has a huge wing-span. Some eagles have wingspans that are as wide as five feet. An eagle looks, seeks, and targets weak and dying things for survival. Why didn't God send Elijah an eagle? Because an eagle is looking for those who are wounded. You know some eagles, the ones who approach you and say, "*Um hmm*, what are you going to do now? You've stood up to your situation. *Now what?* You're hurting now. You shouldn't have done that. I told you what you should have done."

You're thinking, *That is not what I need right now. I need a raven. I need someone who is going to feed me. Where is your meat, eagle? Where is your bread?* Well, eagles don't bring anything. Eagles come to take stuff away. That is how an eagle survives—off of your situation. "I told you she wasn't the one for you!" An eagle survives off of your misery and pain. Are you that eagle? Do you know an eagle? When things start going wrong in the family, your phone starts ringing, spreading gossip or stories. An eagle survives on someone else's weakness, on one who's dying. It is a good thing that God knows all, because if He sent an eagle, we would have felt that we were dying. If I see an eagle, I know something is not right. But while you are waiting, you have to be careful of the eagles that come into your life. Eagles are troublemakers, too. That is how they survive. I know Isaiah said, "They shall mount with wings like eagles" (Isa. 40:31), but he was talking about the eagle's size, not the eagle's characteristics. We shall rise up like the eagle. So while you're sitting by the brook, like Elijah, you must be careful and mindful of the eagles that will come. They always seem to be opposing everything you want to do. I pray to God that you are not among any eagles.

God could have sent a vulture. Vultures are big birds. As a matter of fact, vultures are large black birds. Vultures have a naked head and neck, and they eat dead and rotten flesh. Isn't that awesome? This bird only eats dead and rotten flesh. That alone should get you excited, because when you look up and don't see any vultures, you know you're not dead. You're still among the living. You have not been taken out. Your situation has not taken you out. Another characteristic of a vulture is that they're actually greedy. When we simply go through things in our life, we have to be very mindful and aware of the vultures. Those are people who are with you when it starts, but it seems like you're dying and they want it all. "Well, you know if Joe can't do the job, I'll do it." Vultures set you up or sell you out in front of everybody.

There is just never enough for a vulture. I thank God for not sending Elijah a vulture, because Elijah wasn't dead. If God said it, it'll get done. If God said it, it'll come to pass. I pray that none of us are vultures!

God could have sent a chicken. A chicken is a domestic bird. A domestic bird is one that stays in its safe haven. It will not go outside of the yard for anything. If you're about ready to stand up and do something, don't you dare count on a chicken, because a chicken isn't going to go out there with you. When Elijah got ready to stand up to Ahab, God said, "I have to get you away from here. I have to send you to another place." Chickens will say, "Well, we'll be here when you get back. I can't ride with you. I can't fly with you. I can't go to the next level with you." A chicken's characteristics are cowardly. A chicken could and can fly, but its mind-set will not let it go to the next level. A chicken has wings and feathers just like the other birds. Why can't the chicken fly? The chicken is a coward. He will pump you up and tell you to stand up to your situation—to do this or that. But when it gets hot, the chicken fades off. The chicken will tell you how to get your situation right, but when you look at this person's life—it's not great. These people you have to be worried about, because they'll prime you up and pump you up. And then they will leave you hanging. I know I've experienced them, and they are not going anywhere. But thank God for sending ravens. I'm pointing out these characteristics so that you will be able to identify your raven when it comes. And if you haven't seen one yet, don't worry. They're on their way.

The ravens are coming! That is the next step of getting

me to the next level. Thank God for not sending a chicken, because that is not *it!*

So, what do we have left? God could have sent a hawk. A hawk is a tough bird. It is a predator with strong claws for seizing its prey. This bird has an aggressive or combative or fighting attitude. That's the aggressive/controlling people. Those are the people who are really trying to help you, but they do more harm than good. These people try to help you, but when you don't follow their advice, they get mad at you. You say, "You're a hawk. Go on!" They say, "I'm just trying to help you!" And then you have to explain to them that they're going about helping you the wrong way. They mean well, though. But these people are hawks, and they are very aggressive and like confrontation. They say things like, "You need to tell your boss you're not going to take this," but you know the hawk's way will only create more drama. They're trying to help you, but they don't quite bring the meat and the bread! What they bring is not the proper feeding! That's why God didn't send Elijah a hawk. Now when it's time to go to war, you might need a hawk. We've all been in those situations that we have to use the hawks in our families, and we thank God for sending the hawk at that time. Trust me, when you're going up against something, you don't want a dove. You say, "Lord, send me a hawk because I am about to do battle. I am about to go to war." We have to understand this.

God could have sent an owl. You know the one who says, "Who? Who?" Now, let's look at the characteristics of the owl. It is a bird of prey. All of the birds are birds of prey. All of these birds survive off of something else. But an owl has a large head, a short beak, and short legs. Owls are considered wise. Sometimes an owl is no more than a foot tall, but the head is the most important thing on an owl's body. Owls are those big-headed people that we have in our lives. You know, they're the ones who think they know it all! They can't even fit into some places, because their heads swell up. They're always saying, "Oh, I know this, and I know that." But notice that an owl also has short legs. An owl doesn't stand tall. It doesn't stand up for a lot of things. The owl can't relate to a whole lot of things or people because its head is too big. It knows a lot. That is why the owl is considered wise. You can't tell an owl anything. Why do you think the owl sits up at night alone?

These very people are by themselves because they can't relate to anybody. They know it all. As a result, owls discount everything. You make a suggestion, and an owl turns it down. "No, that won't work. Not that either." I wondered why does an owl say, "Who? Who?" And I realized, it's because he doesn't have anyone to talk to! The definition of an owl often refers to it as being wise and foolish. Scripture states, you can have all of that wisdom and knowledge and still be by yourself.

I hope you're not an owl! It has little legs, which means it doesn't stand tall on principles and character. Who is going to follow little legs? The beak is very important, also. The beak is what carries the food. The owl has the smallest beak. He does not carry a lot of food. He doesn't do a whole lot of feeding. He just eats enough to make his head larger. "I know this. I know that." People hate to see the owl come around, because the owl proclaims to know everything. An owl comes around and you leave. Owls believe everyone is wrong except them.

God could have sent a crow. A crow is a large black bird with a raven's call. It looks and acts just like a raven. As a matter of fact, the crow and raven are first cousins. The crow sounds just like the raven. A crow's function or purpose is to rejoice greatly, especially over another person's misfortune. Have you ever gotten to that point where you thought this person was *it*, that God sent them to you? And God showed you that they weren't *it* at all! You said to yourself, "But I thought they were right for me. We went so far together. We did this together." That person looked like a raven and sounded like a raven, but just was *not* a raven at all! Why? Because they rejoiced over people's misfortunes.

It is sad to say, but in my opinion, a lot of people are with you, just to see and be there when you fall. At work, they're waiting for you to get fired. In your family, they can't wait to hear that you're struggling. These crows can't wait to gather themselves to talk about—you! It looks just like a raven. But I didn't tell you that it feeds and brings meat and bread, because a crow does not do that! We have to be careful to not be fooled and confused into thinking that our crows are ravens! It talks just like one. But it does not act like one, because a raven feeds and encourages you. A crow just wants to talk about you.

I've discovered that sometimes those are the closest people to us. That's why it hurts so much. Why? "Because I thought that this person wouldn't do that. I thought that she wouldn't say that. I thought she was a raven, Lord, but she was a crow!"

Thank God for the raven. The raven is coming! The raven is the largest bird in the crow family. God doesn't just send you any bird. He sent you the largest bird. He didn't send you the little owl or a medium-sized chicken, pigeon, or hawk. Ravens are considered the most adaptable and intelligent of all birds. Now I understand why God sent Elijah the raven. Unlike the big-headed owl, the raven gets along with everybody. That's why God can send the raven wherever He wants to because the raven can blend in wherever God sends him. He can send the raven to the toughest environment, and he gets along just fine. The raven adapts to whatever situation you put it in.

The raven is also the most intelligent. The raven can speak any language on any subject. He communicates with all of the other birds that have been mentioned. If you want to talk finances, health, politics, the raven can talk that. Ravens are a special bird. God sent Elijah a special bird that could give him exactly what he needed. The bird that adapts in whatever situation you put it in.

God will surround you with people who will assist and guide you on to the right path.

These birds are on assignment for you. Ravens have tall, strong legs, so that when they stand up, they are able to endure with you and support you. These birds have strong legs. Legs strong enough to hold you up in whatever you come up against. People who tell you not to give up, because they believe in you. God knew He couldn't send just any bird because Elijah was dealing with a specific situation. Ravens are multifaceted. Ravens give you exactly what you need. If you need confidence, the raven gives it. If you need building up, the raven does it. If you need a push, the raven pushes you. If you're in trouble and need a partner, friend, or mentor, this bird does that, too.

God sends the right bird for the right situation. Here are some additional references:

1. We also know the Scriptures state that iron sharpens iron. Which means God will send people to sharpen your skill level up for new opportunity.

2. There is safety in wise counsel. God will surround you with people who will assist and guide you on to the right path, if you listen and learn.

3. A man who waters will himself be watered. Clearly when you help others in time you too will receive your help. All clearly points to an upward position.

Let's move to the next level!

Everything comes to him who hustles, while he waits.

—Thomas Edison

A relationship with God is the best account you can ever open. The more you put in it the more interest you will gain.

—Ellis Powell

Genius is the gold in the mine, talent is the miner who works and brings it out.

—Lady Blessington

He who has a slack hand becomes the poor, but the hand of the diligent makes rich.

—Proverbs 10:4, NKJV

But you, be strong and do not let your hands be weak, for your work shall be rewarded!

—2 Chronicles 15:7, NKJV

Three

Don't Get
Comfortable

THIS IS SOMETHING we should be getting excited about—getting ready to go to the next level. It has to become a part of you. Are you excited about your dream? Are you excited about delivering your baby? Example: imagine an expecting mother-to-be carrying her baby. They are connected through the umbilical cord. It is through that connection the baby receives all its nourishment from the mother. The baby relies on Mom to feed it all the right foods and drinks. That's why it is so important for a mother to take vitamins to give all the right things the baby needs to develop.

What are you feeding your baby? Are you ingesting the conversations and motivations to feed your dream so that it too may continue to develop? Are you feeding the baby the wrong things and allowing it to not develop fully, or are you not focusing on your baby and allowing your own habits to harm the baby? Have you not disciplined yourself to eat right spiritually and have developed complications, which have now put your dream at risk? Have you conditioned yourself to exercise your faith and your workout plan? Believe me, they both go hand in hand, because the workout is what allows your air intake and blood flow to the baby to continue at a high rate. You have to work on your dream daily, which allows air and blood to flow to it; that is what continues to give your dream life.

Exercise is also vital, because as the dream grows over time, just like a baby it gets heavier and heavier. In most cases, if not monitored, this will cause you to slow down and just about give up. Some people abort due to the fact of not wanting to go through with carrying the extra pounds. *But we must realize that God will not put on us more than we can bear.* For others their dreams become bedridden and there's a higher probability of never having their dream come to pass. Also, make sure to watch out for secondhand smoke, for that can harm your baby. In this case, secondhand smoke is bad advice; since you are in the company of others who have harmed or crippled their dreams, you partake in the fear, doubt, and skepticism. Please be careful, for this too will stop your baby from kicking, jumping, or moving at all.

I read somewhere that a baby knows its mother's voice while in the womb. Wow! That blew me away. Doctors state if the mother reads or talks to the baby, it increases the baby's thinking ability. So in other words, it enhances the baby. Isn't that incredible when you think about it! My question to you is, do you talk to your dream? Are you enhancing your dream? Is it becoming more real to you daily? Are you conscious of it daily? Do you think of what it will be like? Do you think of what it might become one day? I think of mine all the time. *I speak of it constantly, because it reminds me of what to look forward to.* It keeps me focused, and through the tough times I reflect on the day it will be birthed.

Example: At times I act like a bounty hunter setting out to find his fugitive. I know what it looks like, but it seems as though it is not in the place it should be. So I have to go looking for it. So I tell my dream daily, "I'm tracking you down, and I'm getting closer and closer to you." And it seems like when I get focused and start going, I don't know if I'm getting closer to it or it is drawing closer to me. But I do know something, and that is that I'm closing in on it. It seems that my focus, commitment, and work have created

Your prosperity and joy are based on you not getting comfortable, but always seeking your next assignment or dream.

this magnetic force. And daily it seems to attract more things that help me stay on the track of my dream. God will always use the T.I.P.S. phone line to call you and let you know where you should look. Faint not! In time it will show up and surrender! You will capture it and prepare yourself to receive your bounty or reward. Your prosperity and joy are based on you not getting comfortable, but always seeking your next assignment or dream. It seems like the more you want to find it, the more it wants to be found. Scripture states, "Seek, and you will find" (Matt. 7:7). It also states as you draw nigh to God He will draw nigh to you (James 4:8). But you must realize that you must have commitment. You cannot get comfortable going to the next level.

Have you ever seen the Olympics? Or back in junior high school, when you got ready to run track and the announcer says, "On your mark. Get set. Ready. Go!" I hope you're not sitting there getting comfortable in your stance, because you should be getting ready to move. I love when people get hired or promoted within an organization. The employer will say, "Congratulations on your new job or new position." And they'll respond, "Yes, I am so thankful to God for this one, and I'm getting excited for my next one." You can't say that out loud to too many people, because they'll say, "Hold your horses. You should get comfortable." But you shouldn't get comfortable, because this is just the beginning. Remember in the review process they asked you for your one-, three-, and five-year goals. You're on your way to what God has for you. This is just another step. So, we cannot get comfortable. An old wise saying says, "Dress for the job you want, not the job you have." That is *getting ready!* Pessimistic people know it far too well. They'll say, "I don't know what you're coming in to work all dressed up for." But you're dressing for your next promotion. When they see you, they see their next boss. Project the image of the vision. They will see that anointing and favor from God, which brings about success. That's getting ready, not getting comfortable, where you are.

> An old wise saying says, "Dress for the job you want, not the job you have."

Every time the disciples seemed to get comfortable, Jesus did another miracle. Why? He was trying to take their faith to the next level. Be careful not to get too comfortable. The people that we hang with can't get comfortable. Have you ever noticed that when your boss promotes you to management, he or she says, "Look, there are things you are going to have to work on and develop. Now you can't be as close to your coworkers as you used to be, because I've just taken you to the next level." You have to know how to distinguish between the two. You can't get comfortable. If you get comfortable, you'll get caught up.

Who are you running with? Remember, we discussed in the earlier chapter that the ravens are coming! Who are you getting comfortable with?

An old saying goes like this: "I don't have to know anything about you. Just show me who you hang with, and I can tell you all about yourself." *Who are you flying with? Are you hanging with ravens?* The people who are bringing you

> "I don't have to know anything about you. Just show me who you hang with, and I can tell you all about yourself." *Who are you flying with? Are you hanging with ravens?*

meat and bread? Are *you* a raven? Are you always looking to feed someone—whether it is in the mental, the physical or the spiritual? Do you always have a piece of bread or meat to encourage someone? To inspire someone. To motivate someone. To exalt someone.

There are two other birds I want to discuss that God chose not to send to Elijah. The parrot is a semi-tropical bird with a short hooked bill. That bill alone ruled the parrot out. A short bill means he can't carry enough food to where he needs to go. So a parrot can't feed you. A parrot is also known for imitating and repeating mindlessly. I know quite a few parrots who seem to just say a lot of things without thinking about it at all. You know those people to whom you talk. They can repeat and quote everything they have heard. But when you look at them and their lifestyle, they are not living according to the Word at all.

I heard one great quote that said, "I'd rather know one scripture and live it, than to know them all and live none of them." A parrot imitates. He mimics. Parrots say all these things to show you that they know it. But their application shows that they know *none* of it. We're about living it. We're about becoming the Scripture. That is the walk that God wants us to walk, just like His Son Jesus. Let's not hang around these parrots, repeating everything. Parrots are the gossiping folks, too. They repeat everything they hear without asking, "Is it true? Is it kind? Is it necessary?" No thoughts take place at all. Are you with parrots and you're supposed to be with ravens?

A cuckoo bird. What kind of bird is this? Once you read this definition of a cuckoo bird, you will understand why they call this bird cuckoo—not just due to the fact that it has a two-note call that goes *coo-coo, coo-coo.*

But let me show you how cuckoo this bird and some people are. A cuckoo bird is the greatest European bird that lays eggs in other birds' nests. Isn't that crazy? I would call it cuckoo. These birds have birds and leave them in other birds' nests. They rely on other birds to raise their birds or dreams. Let me bring it home. We have a whole lot of cuckoos who are our friends, family members, and even neighbors, expecting other people to raise their baby. Remember earlier we discussed how you should be connected to your dream like a mother is to her baby. Well, these people are asking other people to carry their dream for them. We have folks like that today—abandoning dreams and waiting on other people to make it happen for us!

These people believe that one day out of the blue it will just happen and you don't have to do anything. Trust me when I tell you that it does not work like that at all; anyone who believes that is truly a cuckoo bird. Scripture states that a lazy hand brings about poverty. It is about time that we stand up and take charge over our own eggs/dreams. My life. My future. My family. I'm not going to sit back and do nothing and believe it is going to happen without my participation.

Be a raven! Let me emphasize two additional facts about the raven. The raven will attack owls, hawks, pigeons, crows, and eagles. This bird is the most adaptable and intelligent bird of them all. This is the bird that God sent Elijah. This bird that God sends to you will protect you from all those other birds. You know those people who come to you and say, "Don't pay those people any mind. God is on your side. God is going to do this and that for you." The raven comes to protect you from all of those things that are attacking you.

Did you also know that the raven builds its nest on top of a tree as opposed to in a tree? It seems to me that this raven understands the relationship with God and wants to be closer to God. So the ravens make their homes on top instead of in the middle or below. To the ravens reading this book, I ask: where is your nest?

Where is your home? Is it on top? You see things a lot clearer from the top. Most birds make their home inside the tree. Have you ever noticed that anyone who has been on a hike or exploring, that when you get to a peak, it seems to be peaceful and calm. Because you're on top. You decided to rise above your situation. You get that oneness, that closeness, and that connection with God. Every time the raven moves, he moves his home on top—whether it is on top of a tree or on top of a pole. The raven understands that the only way to go to the next level is to remain on top. Scripture tells me that I'm the head and not the tail; I'm above it and not beneath it. (See Deuteronomy 28:13.) Start making your home, your resting place, on top with God. That is what a raven does. Fly with other ravens, the people who make their homes on top.

Now let's go back to 1 Kings 17. Let's learn from Elijah that we cannot get too comfortable. Notice that people who have a mind-set of expectation are not comfortable. They are getting ready. They always have an attitude of change because they're thinking that they never know when they may have to move. They know that God is a God of promotion. He is a God of taking you from one high to the next high because He loves "blowing our mind." Scripture states that *He exceeds more that we can ask or imagine.* (See Ephesians 3:20.)

I remember one particular position that I had, and they moved me from one office to the next office. I only put up one picture of my family and my clock; I left all of my little degrees and plaques in the box. They asked me, "Aren't you going to hang that up?" I said "Nope, I'm not going to be here too long. I don't want to get too comfortable."

Most folks have all of those pictures and stuff all along the wall. They stay in one office for years. But me, I'm not going to be here too long. I'm already communicating with my future. I'm telling it, "Don't get comfortable; I am coming." So when we go back to 1 Kings 17:6, we discover: "The ravens brought him bread and meat in the morning, and bread and meat in the evening; and he drank from the brook." Now this was the time that he resided by the brook during the three-year drought that he had told Ahab about. The ravens fed him morning and evening. God took care of him, like He takes care of us. Now here is the thing. I do believe that at a certain point Elijah said, "Hey, this is all right. God is handling His business. I kind of like it here. God, I think You've done Your job. This is good enough for me. I am fine here at the brook, drinking however much I want too. Let me be. By the morning, the ravens should be arriving. After I eat, I'll walk around and think about life and its goodness. By evening, the ravens should be showing up again. I'll eat again."

How many of us are like that? "Well, God, life is good. I've got this job, and I don't really want anything else. I've got the house I want. I've got the car I want. My family's doing all right. The bank statement looks pretty good. I'm fine right where I am. I have enough money. I'm all right." This all sounds like someone who is getting a little too comfortable.

How many times have we gotten what we wanted, and we have sat around and have said something silly like, "Well, I have everything I need now. I don't want anything else. I'm fine. If I get this job, I don't want any other job. If I make this much money, that's enough for me. If I get this house, this will be my last house. This is it for me." You're getting too comfortable. You have really pushed God out and said, "There is no need for You anymore. I'm fine." What you did was speak to your future, saying, "There is no need for anything else. There is no need to look forward to anything else in my life. I have all I want."

This makes me think of Solomon, who had everything. Slowly but surely he pushed God away. "I'm fine. I'll talk to You later. If something else comes up, I'll call You. Don't call me, I'll call You." Until things start to go wrong, then you're on the phone again. How can you get ready to go to the next level when you're saying this is *it*? If you have no money, how about $100? If you have a $100, why not $1,000? If you have $1,000, why not $10,000? If you have $10,000, why not $100,000? Why not $1 million? You have a million? That's great; why not ten million? You have one bedroom, why not two? You have two; why not three? Don't we serve a God who desires to bless with abundance?

The beautiful thing about the relationship that we have with God is that God wants to take you to the next level. He wants to promote you. You could never ask enough from Him that He can't deliver. God wants us to rely on Him. If you say this is enough, then you are no longer relying on God. That's the trap we fall in. Sometimes I believe some people think they are helping God out by not asking for anything else.

Let's look at 1 Kings 17:7; there is a revelation that comes in. "And it happened after a while that the brook dried up." You've gotten so comfortable that after a while God wants to get you back to where you were so that He can take you to the next level. Sometimes He has to dry up our brook.

He says, "I've missed you. When the river was flowing and the raven was coming, you didn't need Me anymore. But I love you so much and I love the relationship that we have, and I miss it. You seem to have forgotten about Me or think I have forgotten you. And I want to promote you to the next level, so I'm willing to dry your brook up. If I don't, you won't get to the next level."

I know that sometimes it's difficult when we don't have enough money or our body begins to fail us, and we're going through things in our personal lives with our families. Some marriages experience divorce. Sometimes we get laid off from our jobs. These things are, in essence, our brooks drying up. But get excited because God is going to take that situation to promote you and get you to the next level. There is nothing too big for the God we serve! God says, "I'm willing to use those situations."

Remember when Jesus got the word that Lazarus was sick and the disciples asked, "Shouldn't we go?" Jesus said, "No, we're going to stay here for your sake. We're going to let him die. We are going to let the brook dry up, so that My Father can get all of the glory." Jesus doesn't care about what you lack. Lack isn't bigger than God. It doesn't matter what storms and troubles you are going through in your life or your marriage or with your children, because nothing is too big for God. God needs to dry the brook up to take you to the next level because you were getting a bit comfortable. You were feeling like you had it all made and God shook things up.

God will shake things up! Remember in Mark 4 when the disciples were on the ship sailing across the water and the storm came? The waves began to toss the boat, so the disciples went to wake Jesus. Jesus said, "What's the problem?" The disciples said, "Our ship has been shaken up, and we are about to perish." Jesus said "No, you're not, you of little faith." What He was saying to them was, "I am going to use your situation and take you to the next level!" So we praise Him anyhow, because we know that God the Father who loves us is up to something.

Some of us need our brooks dried up, because God is looking for children who trust and have faith in Him. For forty years, God fed the children of Israel both day and night, because He was looking for them to depend on Him. When He dropped manna on the ground each morning for them to eat, He told them not to pick up any of today's manna for tomorrow. If they did, God told them, "I'll turn the manna into maggots, because I want you to rely on Me." (See Exodus 16.)

The rest of verse 7 in 1 Kings 17 states, "Because there had been no rain in the land." Because there had been no rain, the situation remained the same. Have you ever noticed that things around you can be going bad but it doesn't affect you? There was still no rain, so how was Elijah drinking and eating good? God was providing!

During the recent war, the gas prices have gone up very high. People ask, "What are you going to do about the gas?" I reply, "Nothing, but continue to get me some. God is going to make a way somehow. God will provide even if the prices are going through the roof." The situation around me has not changed, but my reliance upon God has changed. I'm not going to let situations suppress, depress, or oppress me.

The Bible said it still had not rained, but Elijah was still eating and drinking well because the God he served was providing for him. But that wasn't it. The brook dried up because there had been no rain. Uh oh, the water supply is off. No more ravens. But Elijah didn't panic, because he had a relationship with God. Elijah said, "OK, my Father is up to something." If He turned this off, that means He's already turned something else on. If God has closed this door, that means He has already opened another door! That is the kind of God we serve! For some of us, God has to close the door on us to get us to go through the right door. God says, "I'm going to dry this brook up…I'm going to close this door." You ask, "What am I supposed to do now?" He says, "Do what you've been doing. Rely on Me; nothing has changed. I'm going to open up another door." So Elijah did not panic.

Let's look at 1 Kings 17:8 to see what Elijah did. When the situation changed, Elijah went back to God and the relationship he had with God. I'm sure after the ravens stopped feeding him meat and bread he went on a quick fast. The river has dried up, so he's not drinking. The Lord said, "I'm about to humble and consecrate you, for you are going to the next level."

Scripture states, "I can do everything through Him [Christ Jesus] who gives me strength" (Phil. 4:13). I know I can do this because it is God that I lean on. King Solomon wrote, "Trust in the LORD with all your heart and lean not on your own understanding" (Prov. 3:5). It is God that I depend on. It is God that I cast my burdens on because I know He cares for me.

After Elijah fasted and prayed, then the word of the Lord came to him and said, "I've got you now." God says this after Elijah fasted and prayed. "It is just Me and you now. You have tuned out everyone else. You have turned away from your situation and now you're in My presence. I'll talk to you now. First you got a little comfortable. But I've shaken up your situation. Now you've cried out for Me." Then the Word of the Lord came to him.

When you're going through your situations, you should do the same thing. When your situation is shaken up, you should fast and pray. And then the word of the Lord will come to you. That's all I want. That's my true meat and bread. "Lord, all I need is a word from You. If You said it, it is done. If You give me the vision, I know You've already got the provision. I know You *already have it completed and worked out for my good.* If you said it, it is so! I need a word from You. I know the brook is dried up. I know the ravens aren't bringing me the meat and bread.

"Jesus said in Matthew 4:4 that man cannot live by bread alone, but by every word that proceeds out of the mouth of God. I need a word! I need a word from You, God. Once I hear from You, I know I can make it because I know You're with me on this."

Then the word came to Elijah saying those same directions God told him earlier. He's going to another level. So he has experienced this before. Remember, the first time the Lord came to him, He said, "I'm going to take you away from this. Hide and go eastward." God never just tells you to do something *without giving you instructions.*

God is a God of order, not confusion or chaos. You should always call on Him and wait to get a word from Him. And His word will be clear. First Kings 17:8–9 reads:

Then the word of the Lord came to him, saying, "Arise, go to Zarephath, which belongs to Sidon, and dwell there."

In other words, "Lord what do I do now?" "Get up and go to a place I have once again prepared for you." Notice, God gave him a specific place to go. Any other place would be outside the will of God. When you get there, stay there. There are instructions. If you miss out on any of those instructions, you miss out on the blessing He has for you. Remember, when He told him to go eastward to the brook, the ravens were not there yet. So Elijah had to stay there. Here is evidence of the humbleness and patience that God works within us to trust Him. Get there and dwell there! Stay there, until I say so! See? I have commanded the ravens to feed you.

In this case, God is using the same instructions. He wants you to continue to do that same process, over and over and over. That is how we develop practice. That is how we develop habits. And that is how we develop our character.

I go back to the same thing that I did before. He spoke to me then; He'll speak to me now. Verse 9 reads, "I have commanded a widow there to provide for you." Does that sound like the same thing He did with the raven? He said, "I'm still going to take care of you in your situation of need. *I will never leave you or forsake you.* I'm still there. I'm still with you. I've instructed someone to provide for you. I moved you from this situation to that situation, but when you get there, you wait on Me."

We've all had those new jobs or been to a new place and had those situations where someone just walks up to you and says, "Look, I was just led to do this for you." Or, "I just feel like I was ordered or commanded by God to make sure you get what you needed." I know I can attest to that because He has sent ravens for every situation I've been in. For those who are reading this book, I am your raven and you are mine. I thank God because it shows that there is a God who loves us, cares for us, and always sends people in our lives to provide for us. So Elijah arose.

Just getting a word from God is not enough. The other half is doing your part. You are still co-creating. You can get all of the instructions, but if you don't take heed and follow them, none of the things God said will come to pass for you. Verse 10 says: "So he arose and went to Zarephath. And when he came to the gate of the city, indeed, a widow was there gathering sticks."

I love the word *indeed*. It means "surely." Surely, it was the way God said it was going to be. God said she was going to be there, and she was there. Because Elijah followed God's instructions. The second half of verse 10 states, "And he called to her and said, 'Please bring me a little water in a cup, that I may drink.'"

Remember, the brook had dried up. God has not forgotten about that. He knows you haven't had anything to drink, so he sends a person in your life to fulfill those things you need.

What is it you need today? God has ravens/angels to take care of your needs! He has already ordered someone to take care of what you need. He knows our needs before we ask. We don't all need the same thing. But we serve a God who can take care of all of our needs. As a matter of fact, He meets us at our point of need. How badly do you want it? Do you need your need that much? Then follow His instruction.

That's how you go to the next level. You can't get comfortable. Had Elijah stayed at the brook, he would have never met the widow at Zarephath. He would have never had his need met and fulfilled. Don't get comfortable. When God speaks to you and says, "It's time to go," then it's time to go. Do not argue with Him. "Well, I've been at this job for so long. I've been living in this house for so long. I've been going to this church for so long." If God has spoken to you and you've gotten a word, don't argue with Him. Pack up and go! If God told you, then God will bless you, and you should go.

Don't let anyone get in your way and hinder what God has for you. No one knows your needs but God. He can fulfill your needs. No one else can. Are you still in the same situation? Have you gotten comfortable? Has God spoken to you? Have you moved? Are you still at the brook? Are you still hungry? Are you still thirsty? Go! Move! Do what God told you to do. The brook has dried up and you're still there. Your needs will not be met at the brook. It's time to go. Don't get comfortable. Get yourself in position to go to the next level.

My business is not to remake myself, but to make the absolute best of what God made.

—ROBERT BROWNING

An uncommon dream will require an uncommon faith.

—UNKNOWN

I'm a believer in luck and I find the harder I work the more I have of it.

—THOMAS JEFFERSON

Do you see a man who excels in his work? He will stand before kings; he will not stand before unknown men.

—PROVERBS 22:29, NKJV

Many of us spend half of our time wishing for things, we could have, if we didn't spend half of our time wishing.

—UNKNOWN

Four

Don't Look Back

B Y NOW YOU are beginning to understand how God works and are reflecting on parts of your life on how you now sense Him being there. It's like going somewhere and experiencing something totally wonderful or amazing and actually taking a picture of it. Our lives are moments being captured just like photos. Isn't it great going through life snapping away with our camera (minds), looking through the lenses of our eyes, with our thoughts being the flashes that brighten our lives? Once the lens is focused, we snap the picture with our flash on, and it instantly makes a print or image on our minds. Isn't God awesome?

Once the film has been handled with care, then it takes time before the picture becomes clear. It's amazing how pictures taken at an event capture feelings, thoughts, and even people in the background that you didn't even realize were there. I think you see my point—if you reflect on certain moments and times in your life you will see God in the picture. I have several pictures like that in my life. Also, if you look through some of those old pictures of victory, overcoming, and triumph in your life, and you look deep in the background you will find Him in there, preparing and equipping you for the next level.

Let's recap quickly.

1. You must stand up to your situation.

You must fast and pray. You must stand on the Word of God, which means obeying the instructions of God, knowing that He has the power to change your situation. And then you must stand back and watch God in your life, because God will provide.

2. We know that ravens are coming because God has commanded the ravens to feed.

God will send people in your life to provide for you.

3. Don't get comfortable, because God is a God of promotion.

He is going to give you some tests to take you to the next level. Sometimes He will dry up your brook to get you to move to the next level.

Now we want to focus on "Don't look back." It's about the here and now and the future. If God is promoting you to the next level, why are you concerned about the past? Don't worry about your past finances, your background, your past troubles, your education, your failures, and the situations you *were* in. Whether you dropped out of school or made some bad financial dealings; you made some bad choices in life or simply did some things you now regret. That was in your *past*. God is bringing you to a new place in your life. Don't worry about how much you used to smoke or drink. That's in your past. Stop continuing to think about your past, because it is hindering you from stepping into your future. I don't care about how many times you've been married or how many times you've been divorced. I understand that this didn't work and that didn't work, but why are you still harboring those thoughts?

Chances are that your new relationship isn't going to work either! Why? Because you're bringing your old way of thinking into it. *Don't look back!* Quit focusing on "I didn't do this. I didn't do that!" Well, it sounds to me that you're not going to do it *now* either, because you're focusing on those old thoughts. Leave those things behind.

Illustration: A man gets in his car. He puts the key in the ignition and starts the car. After putting the car in drive, he steps on the accelerator. But instead of looking forward, he's looking in his rearview mirror. His intent is to move forward in his life; however, he cannot see what's before him or what lies ahead because he is looking backward! Chances are high that he's going to have an accident.

Most of us continue to have mishap after mishap because we're looking back. Look forward to your future! Go toward that. Don't worry about the past. The past is history, or shall I say your story. Your story is a time in your life that you went through "a tunnel," if you will, that is connected to the bridge called your future!

Why do you continue to torment yourself with that type of thinking? Some people continue to stay in the tunnel, which is dark and does not have much light. But you must continue through! There is always light at the end of the tunnel, and your destiny awaits you! Notice, once you come out of the tunnel there's a bridge! God always has a bridge. A bridge is a structure that provides passage across an obstacle. If you can stay focused and diligent, you will overcome all of those hindrances and difficulties that had seemed impossible to pass. Not only will you not have to go through the deep waters and low valleys to travel to your destiny, but you will also go *over* them. God will always make a way out of no way! Don't despair and become afraid once you have reached close to your edge; your bridge will be there to cross. Remember, don't give up and look back now! We have come too far together on this new journey. You cannot look back if you expect to go to the next level!

In order for you to have something you never had, you must be willing to do something you've never done!

Quit saying, "This is what I used to do." That's your problem. You need to change and do a new thing. Think a new thought! In order for you to have something you never had, you must be willing to do something you've never done! Get some wise counsel to keep you on target. Hang with some ravens!

Let's take a look at horses that run in the Kentucky Derby and other races. Or greyhounds that race. Have you ever noticed that they put those blockers on both sides of their eyes? They do that so they can stay focused. Look at the dogs that run behind the little rabbits around the track. The dog is fixed on the rabbit. The closer the dog gets to the rabbit, the faster the dog runs. Why? Because he knows his purpose, and the rabbit is connected to his reward. The prize in our lives is Jesus, the Word. The closer you get to Jesus, the closer you get to the finish line and the reward He has for you in your life. Are you chasing the rabbit? Are you chasing the Lord?

Just one more illustration. I want to paint a vivid picture as to why you should not look back if you plan on going to the next level. A sprinter in the Olympics or a marathon listens for the announcer to say, "On your mark, get set, go!" The sprinter is pursuing the prize. He is pursuing to win his race. Now, when you're racing and going toward your mark, you must stay in your lane. If you get out of your lane, you're disqualified. Stop trying to compete with everybody else! You're not against everybody else. You're racing against *you*! All you want to do is beat your best time. If you're able to beat your best time, you will be able to win your race.

When a sprinter is running, the coach always tells him *not* to look back, because when he looks back, he takes his focus off of what he is pursuing. The coach also tells the runner *not* to look back, because it also distracts him from the momentum that he has. It's not as if the runners behind him are any faster because he is in the lead. In your race, your own personal life, you are in the lead! The crowd is yelling, "Go! Go! Go!" The coach says, "You are doing great; just don't look back!" The reason for this is because it takes you off focus. It takes your eyes off the prize that you should be running toward! Before you know it, you are now slowing down. You cannot afford to look back. I know you can do it! Let's look at a passage of Scripture:

> Remember ye not the former things, neither consider the things of old.
>
> —Isaiah 43:18, KJV

The New American Standard version reads, "Do not call to mind the former things."

Why are you thinking about the old stuff? *Well, I didn't do this right. I didn't finish…. I made a mistake here. I made a mistake there!* Why are you thinking about those things? The Scripture says do not think of those things if you're getting ready to go to the next level. You cannot afford to do that! If you plan on going back to school, you can't keep telling yourself that you didn't finish or you're too old. Why are you bringing those things up? Those things are in your past. You can't afford to think about, take captive, and hold on to those old things. It is hard for you to grab on to their future when you are still holding on to their past. It is hard for you to step in the future when you're stuck in the past.

Now please beware again of the dream killers I mentioned earlier, because once you stop looking back, you will start to see your life move. Trust me; they will recognize it, too! Again, these individuals are camouflaged as family, friends, co-workers, you name it. When they see that you're committed, they'll say things like, "Well, you know you used to be like this. You used to do that." They're trying to bring up those former things. The Scripture says don't even think about those things.

When those dream killers bring those things up, you should respond, "Yes, I did. But I've moved on." If they continue to bring it up, that is an indicator to let you know they are not on your team. See, we must understand opposition. Opposition is one who opposes you. If I'm trying to go forward and someone keeps pushing me back, then they are my opposition. They say stuff like, "You know you're not this. You know you don't have that. You know you messed up before." You respond, "But I thought you wanted to see me go forward. I thought you wanted to see me go to the next level, but you continually bring up my past." They're your opposition. They are not cheering for you or coaching you. You need to get yourself away from those people because they will stop you from getting to the next level.

The New International Version translates Isaiah 43:18 this way: "Forget the former things; do not dwell on the past." See, I'm doing a new thing! This is a new day. I can't get caught up in yesterday because that is in my past. Whatever I did, I learned from it, and now I want to do a new thing on a new day. I want to be better than I was yesterday. Sure, the opposition—whether Satan or people having satanic/evil ways—wants to keep bringing up what you did or did not do, to keep you from going to the next level. But take no thought of that.

A thought is simply a seed. You must continue to water what you desire to have. You must continue to think over it and the good things you have before you. Remember, your bridge is just ahead. Don't think over your past. Your past is just that. It's your past. I've passed that by. I'm not going to do a u-turn and go back to it! There's nothing waiting for you but that long tunnel through which you have just traveled. There's no telling how long this tunnel may go. Some people never make it out of their tunnel experience. But that's what people want, when they come to you and remind you, "You did this in high school. You just did that two years ago. You said that you would never." God says, "If you forget those former things, then you will be able to do a new thing." (See Isaiah 43:19.)

> A thought is simply a seed.

In order to go to the next level, you must be willing to ignore the dream killers. If God spoke to you and told you to do some things, why are you trying to make or prove your case to everyone else? He didn't show everyone else. He showed you. He didn't tell them. He told you. A lot of times when we're trying to make our case we say, "Just forget it." And we give up on proving our case/purpose/destiny because we can't get anyone to believe us. Not realizing it, you miss out on what God has for you and your future. Why? Because you allowed your past to take a stronghold on you! You cannot do a new thing until you're ready to let go of the old thing!

It's like you wanted to make $15 per hour when you were making $14, and later you started earning that. But if you want to make $16 per hour, you have to let go of the $15. It's that simple! Once you get to $16, trust me, you'll look forward to getting to $17. And it goes on and on and on.

In the last chapter we discussed not getting comfortable. If you get comfortable, you can't get what God has for you. I've been married now going on fourteen years. And I'm fighting for the fifteenth. Whatever happened thirteen years ago is thirteen years old! We cannot continue to take captive of those old things in the past. "Well, I've failed at this. I had a bad relationship in the past. I had a bad marriage. I did some bad business deals. I did this wrong." Well, if you continue to think about that, you're going to continue to make those same mistakes. Don't think about that old stuff. Think about new things.

The first thing you can do with the new thing is let go of the old thing. You will inherit the new one by default.

See, I'm doing a new thing! Now it springs up; do you
not perceive it?

—Isaiah 43:19, niv

If you stop going the old way and take a new route,
you have a whole new direction. God says, "Do you not
see that you're not going the same way you used to go?"
Why? Because you're not thinking the old way you used to
think. You're better off. But do you see it? Your destination
is northbound but you are traveling west and wondering
why you haven't arrived yet. Stop going that way, and go
a different direction! When most people are lost, the last
thing they want to do is pull over and ask for directions. I
have no problem with that because I need to get where I'm
trying to go. Don't worry about those old things!

The whole point is that you are trying to get to your
future. You're trying to get to your next level. God said, "Are
you not recognizing that if you stop doing this, by default,
you're doing something new?" If I just stop doing the old
stuff I was doing, am I doing the new thing?

Yes, you're different. Just like that, you're different! And
that's what we're all about. Now you're getting ready to go
to the next level. Now you're getting ready to connect to
your future. Why? You have let go of your past. Who cares
that you and your spouse argued last week or argued last
year? You stop bringing the arguments up. You continue
to bring the arguments up, and you're going to continue
to argue. It's that simple. And you're wondering why your
marriage is on the rocks. That's why. Sure you've made some
bad business deals. Now you've learned from those deals
and you're saying, "I'm not going to do those business deals
anymore." But don't get stuck on those bad deals, because

73

that will hinder you from doing any new good deals.

Regarding all of your bad situations—think of those things, learn from those things, and don't do those things anymore. You're better off! You're doing a new thing now! "I was with this lady (or I've been with this guy) for so many years of my life, and no one wants me." Learn from that! Whatever your part was (in destroying that relationship), please do not do that anymore! Being wise and embracing your past allows you to watch your future get brighter! Sadly, most people continue doing the same thing because they don't see it. That's why God asked, "Do you not perceive it?" People just don't see it. Therefore if they don't see it, then they don't get it simply because they have nothing to hold on to.

You need to take a stance today and say, "Today is the day I stop it!" When you take that stance, you're doing a new thing. Do that new thing physically. Do that new thing spiritually. Do that new thing financially. Do that new thing socially, with relationships. Do that new thing in your marriage. If you've never saved any money, start today. Even if it's just a $1, you are now on your way! Even though you've been going to church, take a step and do the new thing today! Get connected, join, and be a part of the church. That can change everything!

Isaiah 43:19 continues, "Now it springs up; do you not perceive it? I am making a way in the desert and streams in the wasteland" (NIV). You were in a dry place and saw no way out. Most people die when they're in the desert. Many die because there was no water. But I believe many die long before that because they give up hope. And as they look as far as the eye can see, they lose faith. Most die because they don't see a way out of the desert. So they stay in it. Not because they want to, but I believe most turn back. Instead of pressing on and believing sooner or later there has to be a well, spring, or a sign of life ahead, they spend the same amount of time and effort heading back the way they just came or simply stopping. They don't reflect on the miles they have already traveled.

How many deserts are we in simply because we're not letting go (we continually look back)? We continue to wander and stay lost in it. If I'm in the desert and I know I have a day or two of travel, though the water isn't there, I will get through. But if I stay in the desert five or six days, I'll die. And that's where we are in our lives. We go through these deserted places in our lives and continue to wander because we lack the instructions of a new thing. We're holding on to our past. We continue to make four lefts. Make a left here. Make a left here. Make a left here, and make a left here. And we're right back where we started.

Let go of that. Take a right for a change, and see what happens. I guarantee you will not be in the place where you were at first because you did a new thing. You didn't look back. When people approach you and say, "I remember when you did this," be confident and bold and tell them, "I'm doing a new thing now." How are you doing a new thing? You're doing a new thing because you're not doing that old thing anymore. If someone reminds you, "I remember when you didn't have anything," you tell them, "Yeah, I didn't have anything. But I'm doing a new thing, and now I have a little something and in time I will have much more."

> Brethren, I count not myself to have apprehended:
> but this one thing I do, forgetting those things which
> are behind...
>
> —Philippians 3: 13, kjv

Brethren means Paul is talking to everyone. Paul says, "If you're going to get to the next level, this one thing you must do: Forget the past!" If you continue to think about that, then you're in the past, and you can't live in the past. You can't do a new thing while continually doing old things. Paul says to forget about that old stuff. Forget about the bad marriage. Learn from it, but forget about what transpired. Forget about the bad investment. It was a bad deal and you lost money. Learn from it, and then forget about it. Get ready for a new deal. Get ready for a new relationship. Get ready to make a new commitment now.

Paul only mentioned one thing. If you forget about your past, then you can go into your future. Most people won't get to their future because they keep bringing up their past. They're hanging around people who continually remind them of their past. And they're wondering why they're there yet. They're wondering why they're still in a deserted place. The deserted place is your past. Come out of there or you will surely die. We are to forget what is behind and strain toward what is ahead.

I'm reaching for what is before. I'm going for something that is before. How can it be before? Because your future is not actually after your past but before it. You see, it was there the entire time, but I had to go through my past to understand my present to realize my future. Your future was already outlined for you. But since you stay stuck in the mud in the "after," you don't get what's before you. Healing is before you. Prosperity is before you. Love is before you. Peace is before you. It lies ahead of you. It waits for your arrival. It's just on the other side.

This is not your final destination. You must strain. You must press toward your future! How bad do you want it? How bad do you want that degree? How bad do you want a better marriage? Are you willing to strain because there is a good marriage right before you? Are you willing to break through this?

How badly do you want to lose weight? Are you willing to strain pass that chocolate cake and those buffet tables? That which you so desire is ahead of you. It's there. How badly do you want it? How badly do you want a marriage? If you strain and press, it's just on the other side. How badly do you want it? People who are willing to get to the next level are asking, "Is that all I have to do?"

Paul said, "Just do this one thing—forget your past." Don't be around people who keep bringing your past up. If they're bringing your past up, they oppose you. They don't want you to get to that which is before you. All of the goodness is before you—not after you! Your past is after. I had to go through the after to get to the before. That's God talking, because in our terms, it doesn't make sense. We want the before to come first.

That's why God says, "My thoughts are not your thoughts, nor are your ways My ways....For as the heavens are higher than the earth, so are my ways higher than your ways, and My thoughts than your thoughts" (Isa. 55:8–9). God does things totally different to show us that it is Him, and not us. So we must do, press, and stretch towards those things that are *before* us, forgetting what is behind and straining toward what is ahead. I press on towards the goal to win the prize for which God has called me heavenward in Christ Jesus.

> I press toward the mark for the prize of the high call-
> ing of God in Christ Jesus.
>
> —PHILIPPIANS 3:14, KJV

I press toward this. Or, "Seek ye first the kingdom of God, and all these things shall be added unto you" (Matt 6:33). All that you desire, the love, peace, joy, finances, health, wealth, and good relationships will be given to you if only you are willing to press toward the mark. The closer you get to the mark, the closer you get to what you desire. God has said in His Word that He will give you the desires of your heart. (See Psalm 37:4.) He wants to do it. He's willing to do it. He's able to do it because He loves you. But He wants to see how much you love Him. I think it's a fair trade off. In order to get to the next level, you cannot afford to look back. Otherwise you will lose what's ahead. Your prize awaits you. Stay focused, because your coach Jesus says, "You can do it because I live in you!" I will see you at the finish line.

The future belongs to those who believe in the beauty of their dreams.

—Unknown

Following the word of God is like a bank CD that matures one's life in time.

—Ellis Powell

Following the word of God is like stock, when invested it produces a return and yields a great profit.

—Ellis Powell

But Jesus said to him, "No one, having put his hand to the plow, and looking back, is fit for the kingdom of God."

—Luke 9:62, NKJV

But let him ask in faith, with no doubting, for he who doubts is like a wave of the sea driven and tossed by the wind.

—James 1:6, NKJV

Five

LOOKING BACK WILL COST YOU

I F YOU ARE still with me then you are definitely serious about going to the next level. You have made much
progress thus far. If you think I'm not serious, then reflect
on how far you have come, and you will realize that you are
a long way from where you started. But I also have great
news to share with you. You can smile now! You are half
way there! It is very important that you note your progress
and commend yourself because, believe it or not, you are
moving forward.

So let's continue to walk together on this journey. If I
may add this quick thought before we dive into this next
chapter: *You have to change.* Change starts with you. People
can change without growing, but people can't grow without

changing. In other words, people can change from bad to worse and things not get any better because they have simply stunted their growth. Change has to take place for you to grow. Growth is vital to your success!

When a hiker is hiking or climbing a mountain, there is a series of things that are happening to this individual. First, the arms start to bulk and form from the reaching and stretching toward their goal. Not to mention when things fall down on them from above, they might have to grab hold of the rock along their path. Trust me! If you are climbing, sooner or later you're going to have to grab hold of your rock. My Rock is Jesus, who is the Creator of All. When life seems to blow its heavy winds my way or the enemy throws things my way, Jesus is what I grab hold of so I won't fall off my path.

> Change starts with you. People can change without growing, but people can't grow without changing.

Second, notice the legs get stronger due to the fact you are going higher and on an incline. You will need these legs because the will (faith) has to become firm when you take your stance or position on what you desire. Until you do that, the legs will not get any bigger. Along the path watch your footing. The reason for this is that there is always some loose dirt/gravel that will cause you to slip and fall. This is important, because most people get here and either get hurt really bad or slide further back. Be cautious of this loose dirt, because it is not enough to support you! It is a group of little rocks (negative people) that is not even together, but surround themselves with each other to build a seemingly support system for each other. Remember, these small rocks can inflict pain. How so? They cause cuts, bruises, fractures, and even broken bones. These things have stopped many from reaching their dreams and going to the next level. Keep close to Him who is able to keep you from falling. But for those who watch their steps and hold on to their rock, they will develop a new shape. This is new character! So, you must change! If you don't grow, it will cost you.

Let's look at another scripture: Genesis 19:15. The prior verses are about Sodom and Gomorrah. The Lord had come down and spoke with Abraham. God had said, "I've come down to check out the outcry that I've heard from the people. I come to see for myself." When you call on God, He will come down to see what you have going on. In other words, when a parent has a child and the child is trying to tell you about what happened, but can't quite make it out in words, the parents often will take the time out to go and check it out, and they'll make the judgment call for themselves.

We serve that same type of God. You don't have to worry about anybody lying about you, because God is going to check it out for Himself. God will make the call when He sees it. Remember, He knows all and He hears all. Verse 15 is about Lot, Abraham's nephew. Lot came out of the city Ur when Abraham listened to the word of God. He came out of Ur with his uncle Abraham, who was named Abram at the time, and his aunt Sarah when God called. It's a beautiful thing being connected to the people of God, because when they're hearing God and being obedient, you get blessed, too.

A lot of people are just blessed because they hang around blessed people. God didn't call Lot. He called Abraham. But since Lot understood that his uncle was hearing, listening, and obeying the word of God, Lot went with Abraham and was blessed, too. The bottom line of this story between Lot and Abraham is that both of the men had so much wealth and riches that it was blending and mixing between the two.

The other herdsmen and shepherds were arguing amongst each other, because Lot and Abraham had so much. There was not enough land for the both of them. This was truly an overflow blessing where whoever is a part of you will be blessed as a result. God had told Abraham in Genesis 12:3 that He would bless those who blessed him and curse those who cursed him. That is a covenant that God has provided for us—that HE will pour out a blessing so we will not have enough room to receive it. (See Malachi 3:10.) Illustration: Have you ever had a cup of coffee where it took you a while to fill it up as you were pouring, but the minute it reached the top it started to spill over and run everywhere? Anything and everything that was around that cup pretty much got wet. That is exactly what happened here and what can happen to you.

The cup is your life, the coffee is God's blessings, and the anything/everything are the people in your life. You have to continue to keep your life open for God and only God, because He wants to pour Himself into you. Within Him are love, peace, joy, wisdom, and riches. You must understand that you may open yourself up to other things, but God is the only One who can fill you up and create an overflow! The psalmist David said in Psalm 23 that his cup "runneth over." He had received the overflow and the anointing of God.

That is the type of awesome God I serve—that He, in fact, had blessed both Abraham and Lot because they both served Him. So they had to split up, and Abraham told Lot, "Look, nephew, this is causing too much bickering. We can't have this among family. We love each other. We're going to have to split up. You take one way, and I'll take another way. And I'll let you pick the first direction. You can go east or west." (See Genesis 13.) Lot looked at the east and the west; he saw that one direction was better than the other, so he took what he saw was the better one. That was over by Sodom and Gomorrah. Sodom and Gomorrah was a city of wickedness and evilness, full of ungodly people.

We still have these ungodly pockets today, in businesses, churches, neighborhoods, cities, states, and nations. It's the same thing. But Lot was making so much money off of these ungodly people that he did not want to leave Sodom and Gomorrah. We see that Lot continued to go to the next level. He went away from his rock and rested on the gravel. He went from being cautious to being content. We see that it is just a matter of time before the gravel will give way and cause Lot to slip and fall.

In Genesis 14 we read that people from Sodom and Gomorrah were captured by King Cherdorlaomer, and Lot and his family were slaves. Understand, when you get comfortable around evil and wicked people you have a falling. Not only have you fallen, but also now you will be overtaken by your selfish desires. You no longer stand firm on principle and character, but you now compromise your integrity. Sooner or later this will prove to be painful. Nevertheless, God uses Abraham, a man of God (a raven), to go and rescue Lot. Once again God loves us so much that He sends someone in our lives to deliver us from our situation. (God will always send a raven to help you.)

When Abraham rescued Lot, he asked Lot to come back with him and to prosper together as they had done before. But Lot said, "No, uncle, I'm going to go back to where I was." Lot went right back to the situation that he was in, and it cost him.

Let's learn from Lot. In Genesis 18, we read where God had come down and spoken to Abraham. Abraham said, "Surely, you won't smite the righteous with the wicked?" (See verse 23.) God said, "No, if I can find fifty righteous people, I won't do it. If I can find forty people…thirty…twenty…I won't do it." God got all the way down to ten people. If he could find ten righteous people, He would not destroy Sodom.

The angels went to Sodom and Gomorrah and told Lot what was going to happen.

> When the morning dawned, the angels urged Lot to hurry, saying, "Arise, take your wife and your two daughters who are here, lest you be consumed in the punishment of the city."
>
> —GENESIS 19:15

The Word of God spoke to Lot and urged him to leave his situation, the people, and his surroundings. If you're going to get to the next level, you must remember that there is going to have to be a change. There is going to have to be a sacrifice. You can't think your old thoughts anymore. Some of the old people you used to hang with, you can't hang with them anymore. Some of the old places you used to go, you can't go anymore. God is trying to take you to the next level, but He has to separate you from the ungodly. He has to purify you. He's trying to get you ready to go to the next level. When God speaks to you this time, His message is, "THE TIME IS NOW! The soil is blessed. The door is open. The season is NOW!"

When I started writing this book, I knew "I had to do this now. If I didn't, then I would never do it." I knew the time was NOW! The time was at hand. God had sent his angels and they told me, "You need to hurry! You need to hurry! If I don't get you out of the situation that you're in now, you will never get to the level I have for you."

> When God speaks to you this time, His message is, "THE TIME IS NOW! The soil is blessed. The door is open. The season is NOW!"

Have you ever felt that burning desire or passion? You feel like, "If I don't do this, I am going to die. Things are not going to go right if I don't get this paper finished…get this job completed…get this book finished…lose this weight today. If I don't do it today, I'm never going to do it." That is the Spirit of the Lord urging you, saying, "HURRY!" The place where you need to go is already blessed. If you wait, you're going to miss its season, and when you do get there later, the blessing is gone. The anointing is gone. It does not stay there always. It's a season and time that He has set for you.

There is a season that He has set forth in your life regarding school, jobs, marriage, prosperity, sound mind, peace, and happiness. There is a season He has blessed already. God is saying, "I have to get you out of your old situation and get you over here." It's hard to step into your future when you're stuck in your past! You can't get there. You're stuck. You can't get to something new when you're thinking old. Stop bringing up all that old stuff. Get to the new. Experience the new! You're trying to go to a new place, so quit bringing up yesterday! Why? Don't stay stuck in yesterday. Don't let anyone keep you stuck in yesterday. Get out of that rut! How many opportunities and blessings have you missed because you didn't approach it with urgency?

THE TIME IS NOW! If God speaks to you, THE TIME IS NOW! If there is a stock out there and someone gives you a great tip saying, "This stock is about to increase tremendously," and you feel the anointing of God say, "You better invest right now," THE TIME IS NOW. God sends people in your life and you're thinking, "If I can just get a break…if I can get one opportunity." He's sending people, and if you act now, it will change your whole future. Don't come in with that old way of doing business, that old way of thinking, or that old way of speaking in order to experience a new thing. God answers all.

Don't compare the old to the new! A lot of people make mistakes comparing the old and the new. That's the problem. Experience a *new* thing! Don't you feel worthy of something new? Haven't you had enough *bad* in your life? Keep walking and praying and believing until you experience something new. We know that everyone isn't bad. So if you've had your share of bad people in your life, you're due for some good people.

Go meet some new people! And when you meet the new people, don't use your old way of thinking and deal with them in the same manner you dealt with the bad people. The good people will leave you alone because you haven't changed your thought pattern. You haven't changed how you speak. Experience the new! Expect something new. When God says, "Move," then move, because the time is now. He is able to deliver you out of every situation, affliction, pain, lack, and brokenness. God says, "I have something for you, but you have to move NOW!" If you have kids, think about when you ask them to bring you a glass of water. They start dragging and moving slow. They messed that up. The anointing was NOW. Move now, and the things God has prepared for you, you will receive. If you don't move now, He'll get someone else to bring the water, and they will get what God had for you! God may say, "You missed yours. I was about to bless you, but you didn't make it urgent."

There are so many people walking around here with stuff you could have had. The Word of the Lord spoke to you, but you didn't move. So God used somebody else. Be about your Father's business. When God speaks, you move. That's how I teach and raise my kids. I say, "Bring me a glass of water. Prepare my plate. Wash this up." I want to see them move because I can make things happen in their lives. I'm just looking for some obedience. And that's all our Father is looking for, some obedience. He comes down to the land, seeking men's hearts. He's looking for people He can trust. He's looking for those who are not going to drag all of the time.

Let's learn from Lot. If you don't move into your blessings, you will miss them. Stop hanging around those old folks. Do you know what I mean by *old folks*? Those people who say, "Do you remember five years ago? Do you remember ten years ago?" They are trying to bring you back to the old. You have to say, "Oh, no, you don't. You're trying to bring me back to where I was. You're trying to talk about the old things and start reminiscing." But when you say, "Oh, yeah, I remember," they're thinking, *Gotcha!*

Those persons are not trying to leave the old. "He hasn't changed." You can't entertain those "old" people in those "old" conversations anymore. When they ask, "Why don't you meet us over there? We won't be there long." You must reply, "I don't go to those 'old' places, anymore." How much do you want the new thing? You have to want the new thing so much that you're willing to let the "old" thing go. When the "old" people say, "Girl, I don't see you anymore," you should reply, "You're not in the places I go." If you're on the same level, you should run into each other all the time.

When you were on the same ungodly level, you ran into each other all of the time. You were on the same level. But you're no longer on the same level. You must commit to staying away from your past until you get what's in your future. Once you get what is in your future, you can go back to your past and show those "old" folks how awesome God is. Until then, the "loose gravel" will hinder you from the blessings God has in your future. The "old" people will be no good for you, and you will be no good for the "old" people.

If you're stuck in the past, you're no good to yourself or

the "old" people, because the "old" people aren't trying to get anywhere. You can't miss out. Forget all of the old stuff. Don't let anybody hold you back! People try to hold you back when they bring up your past. They will try to shackle you and overtake you, like Lot. And you should already know that whoever the Son set free is free indeed! So now that you have been freed from slavery, why do you want to go back? Some would say, "I liked it better there. At least we didn't have to scuffle and work hard." But you're a slave again. In order for you to get to the next level, do not get comfortable. A slave mentality is comfort in bondage. A slave may not work hard for anything because everything is there, but a slave will never own anything, either. You're going to have to work. If you want a great marriage, I suggest you roll up your sleeves and get to work! It doesn't come naturally.

Everyone who is married knows it doesn't come naturally. How bad do you want it? You're thinking at times, *Everyone else does not have these problems.* Have you checked with everyone else? How are you going to bring up someone else's problems? What about your problems? There are only two people in the marriage. How badly do you want it? You're thinking that Mary and Johnny don't go through this in their marriage, but are you at home with Mary and Johnny? What happens when the garage door goes down? You don't really know what goes on in that house. Sure, they're going to talk calm and sweet in front of you. But they may curse each other out when they get home. And you certainly do not want what they have!

God came to Lot and told him, "Hurry and take your wife and your two daughters." He didn't just come and get

Lot. When He blessed Lot, He blessed Lot's entire family. That is why family is so important. God has blessed the family. That is one particular institution that God blessed from the beginning. God is a family—God the Father, God the Son, and God the Holy Spirit.

Some families won't even support each other. But what if you knew you were connected to your family? What if you knew that your life, your survival, and your next level were dependant and impacted your family?

If I knew that my livelihood was built upon my brother making it, then it is my job to make sure that my brother gets there. If he gets there, I get there! It is so sad that Joseph's brothers in the Scriptures didn't realize that. They had a brother who made it all the way to the top, but they didn't realize that when he got to the top, they were going to go to the top, too. You must get connected to your family and know that when God takes one of us, He takes all of us.

When we're connected, we leave no one behind. If a tornado comes and pulls me up, and we're all holding hands, then everybody is gone! That's how it is in the body of Christ. When Jesus comes back, if everyone is connected as many members of one body, then everybody has to go. But this happens only if you're connected to one another. The Scripture says if two are in the fields, one of them will still be there (Matt. 24:40). Why? Because they were not connected. You need to be connected. If you don't have a church home or church family, then you're not connected. I want to be connected. That "connection" gives me insurance and assurance. I know this, and I know I have to go. If Jesus comes back right now, I'll be gone, because I am connected. God is going to give you some time to get connected.

We know that when God blesses you, He blesses your entire family. He urged Lot to "arise, take your wife and your two daughters" (Gen. 19:15). Take your family with you into your destiny and your future. Don't move into your future and leave your family! That is not of God. If a husband gets a promotion, it should affect the wife and the children. If a wife gets blessed, it should affect the husband and the kids. If the children get blessed, it should affect the mother and the father.

Where does this "mine" mentality come from? It sounds so selfish. The angels came to Lot. The blessing came to Lot, but the angels told Lot to get his wife and his daughters. If God blesses me, I'm supposed to take that and get my family and church family, too. If we're connected, whatever flows on me should flow on everyone else. If a husband is blessed, it should flow onto the wife and children. Everyone should get blessed.

Too many people are getting blessed and saying, "This is mine." Then God no longer trusts them. When you do that, you're disconnecting yourself. God blessed you so that you would bless everyone else. God says, "Go get your wife and your daughters." Don't leave anyone behind who is connected to you! Lot had sons-in-law whom he told to come with him, but they didn't believe Lot, so he had to leave them.

When the Word of God speaks to you, you have to go on. Leave behind those people who aren't listening. Your destiny awaits you! When that loose dirt states, "I don't know why you're going back to school. I don't know why you're spending all of your time writing a book. I don't know why you're spending all of your time going to church. I don't know why you're spending all of your time sending resumes for a job. I don't know why you're starting a new business." Your answer should always be: "Because I know my future awaits me!"

You have to leave those people behind because they're not connected. If I make my business about your business and you make your business about my business, then we're connected. It's our job to make others succeed.

Nothing is more powerful than the Word of God. You must take the Word, receive the Word, and build upon the Word. That's your rock. Hold on to it! Illustration: A math teacher teaches young students that two plus two is four. That's the truth. It will never change. But if a student does not comprehend the principle and apply it, then that student struggles in math. Life is our math class. God does not want you struggling in life. The reason the child struggles is that the child doesn't understand. That is why in Scripture it states, in all of your getting, get an understanding (Prov. 4:5, 7). The light goes off when you understand. "Oh, I understand now; if I'm going to have a better new relationship, I can't do any of the old stuff."

In the second half of Genesis 19:15 God says, "You take your wife and your two daughters who are here, lest you be consumed by the punishment of the city." I've read that many times and didn't get it. But God is saying—unless you leave your situation...stop thinking those things you used to think...stop going to places you used to go, your old situation is going to consume you. How about this? That is your punishment. You won't see any of the good stuff God has for you because you cannot let the old stuff go. That's your punishment! I told you it was going to cost you! God says, "If you don't take heed to the word that I am speaking to you, and if you don't move right now, then you're going to stay stuck in your situation." That's God! And it makes so much sense. God is saying if you don't want to listen to Him, then He'll just leave you where you are. You could have gone, but since you didn't take heed to God's Word, then stay stuck where you are. That's your punishment.

Parents use the same discipline with their children all of the time. Since they were disobedient, they will not go out to the restaurant, event, or any extra activity. "You stay here at home; we'll be back." That's their punishment or chastisement. You don't see any of the sights; you don't get a chance to have fun today. You get a chance to listen to everyone else talk about how much fun he or she had. Everyone else is talking about how good the Lord was to him or her, but your hard head wouldn't move. You couldn't break away from the old stuff. You're disobeying God if God has called you to the next level and you're not moving.

It is so good when one graduates in the school of higher learning—to go to the next level. But understand that when you graduate, school is never over. You should continue to learn new things to prepare you for the next level!

Most people just want a job. They are not promotion-minded at all. Some people just want to finish high school. They are not degree-minded at all. They are not entrepreneur-minded, at all. Paul said we should be leaving that elementary teaching and move on to maturity, the next level. There is always a next level. Your finances can always get better. Your marriage can always get better. Your mind-set can always get better. Your body and your health can always get better. So that means there is always another level. People stay focused on being so gradual, so cordial. "There's always room for improvement." That means there is room for another level. We have so much here.

And while he lingered…

—GENESIS 19:16

Lot lingered. That showed that he was not confident or convinced. The angels had to drag him. He's not quite sure that if he does this, it will pay off. He's dragging. He's pouting. He's a bit reluctant. We're talking about when the Word of God has spoken in your life and told you to do this and you began to drag or delay. Your future is not going to wait on you that long. There is something called "a door of opportunity." It swings open and it swings closed. The Lord speaks to you and says, "It's open!" You should run like crazy. You should run as hard as you can because now you understand your purpose.

Once you understand your purpose, you should use the other four *p's*:

1. *Passion*—that is the emotion that will pull you through the tough times and push you past the bad.

2. *Power*—God will indwell you with His Spirit because it is His will for your life.

3. *Patience*—Understand it will take some time, but God's Word will come to pass.

4. *Priority*—this must take precedence over everything else in your life because God sent it. It is highly important, and it is valuable money. It is your main objective and will require focus.

The apostle Paul said, "I press on, and I strain on to reach the marker before me, to reach that prize." Your door is open. Promotions. Good health. Prosperity. Peace. Love. The door is open. Run *to* it! Run *through* it! Don't drag. Right now someone is reading this and saying, "This is all I'm going to do." Then you're not going to get it! You keep asking for a better relationship or a better spiritual awakening or awareness, but this is all you're going to do. You've already told your future that you're not going to act right. Then that's it. There is no need to expect anything more. There is not another level with you. This is it! There is no reason to look for anything new. I can tell you your future at this point, and I do not even need a crystal ball. Are you ready? Here we go. Where you stand is where you're going to be tomorrow. Thought: Show me what you are working on today, and I will show you your future tomorrow. That's it. There is no next level for you. You've spoken it. You have to be aware of saying those old things, speaking those old thoughts, dealing with those old people, and going to those old places.

Show me what you are working on today, and I will show you your future tomorrow.

Lot is lingering and dragging. The Word of God has told him to hurry up. The door is open. You can do this. And he is dragging, like God is bothering him. But he didn't understand what was coming. God had told him that he was going to destroy Sodom and Gomorrah. But he didn't understand that God was going to take him to the next level. He couldn't see the other level, and that is why he was dragging.

Your kids see no reason to do these things for you because they don't believe that there is another level or reward from you. Illustration: a borrower of money. Most people don't pay the lender back the money they owe because they don't see the other level. Trust me, if I borrowed $100 from you and paid you back, then I think I will earn enough credit to come back later and borrow $200. There is another level! If I paid you back $200, I don't think you'll have a problem with me asking for $500. There is another level! But if I don't see it, then I don't pay back the first $100 because I don't see that I can get anymore from the person who let me borrow the money.

"Why should I do right on this job? I'm probably not going to get another job out of them." You spoke it. You believe it, and you already have it. You're right; you won't get anything else from these people. That is why we are told to do our best at all things, because we expect all things great to happen to us. Romans 8:28 reads, "And we know that all things work together for good to those who love God, to those who are the called according to His purpose." There is a condition: for those who love the Lord. The only reason I do well is because I love Him. That's His standard…His excellence. Do your best. Anyone who says, "This is all I'm going to do," I don't think that's your best. "This is too hard." Well, this isn't on you. Nothing is too hard for God. But I guess you're not connected because you're only seeing what you can do. But it's not on me and what I can do.

Because I can do all things through Christ, who strengthens me, I'm connected. If I give Him just a little something to work with, He will do the rest. Give Him two pieces of fish and five loaves of bread, and watch Him feed five thousand men, plus women and children. Save a couple of dollars, and watch Him bless that. Say a few kind words to your spouse, and watch Him bless that. It's not just on you. You just have to give him a little something that He can work with. Show God some effort.

It's just like a struggling student with the teacher. The teacher just wants the student to give a little something she can work with. Show some effort. "I'll come in early. I'll stay late. I'll come on weekends. Just show me something." We have a Father who says, "I'll take you to the next level. Don't start dragging." This is your future, don't forget that. How badly do you want it?

Lot lingered. He was dragging really slowly. Call it procrastination. You know we get like that sometimes. Someone has spoken to us and said, "Give your life to Jesus," and we start dragging, saying, "I don't know." God says, "Give your tithes, 10 percent of your gross," and we start dragging, saying, "I don't know." God says, "Join that great church; the Word of the Lord is there," and we start dragging, saying, "I don't know." God says "Do your best at work because there is a promotion for you," and we start dragging, saying, "I don't know."

That window of opportunity will not always be there. God is blessing you now, so give Him something to work with, and He will open up the windows of heaven! You don't know if today is your last day here. Consider the rich man who decided to tear down his barn and build a whole new barn. He didn't realize that night was his last night. The psalmist said, "This is the day the LORD has made; we will rejoice and be glad in it" (Ps. 118:24). You must take every day as if it's your last day. Anything can happen, but if you're connected and have the insurance and the assurance, then you're OK!

Be not simply good, but good for something.
—Thoreau

I find the great thing in this world is, not so much where we stand, as in what direction we are moving.
—Goethe

The whole secret of a successful life is to find out what it is one's destiny to do, and then do it.
—Henry Ford

The end of a thing is better than its beginning; The patient in spirit is better than the proud in spirit.
—Ecclesiastes 7:8, NKJV

Do you not know that those who run in a race all run, but one receives that prize? Run in such a way that you may obtain it.
—1 Corinthians 9:24, NKJV

Six

HEAD TO THE TOP
(MOUNTAINS)

LET'S GO FORWARD with a quote I have prepared for
you. It is, "Think on these things." What to remember?
What to forget?

It seems to me that the good things, the heavenly guidance, and the help that other men have given us to keep on
the right path are the things to remember. The mistakes,
the false leads, and the devilish influences are the things to
forget. Just forget them. Otherwise, if you don't, they will
hold you back from your destiny. They will hold you back
from reaching the next level!

Don't hang around people who always want to bring up
what you did years ago. They are holding you back. You've
heard the old saying about the old crabs in a bucket. Those

crabs are trying to pull you down, knowing that you have a God that is there ready to reach for you and bring you out of your situation. But you have to let them go. Now, I didn't say forget about them. Get what God has for you, and then you can come back because your testimony will be that much stronger. They will believe because you've reached that level that God has for you. Until then you will never get there, and they will never believe. When getting ready to go the next level, looking back will cost you. My daddy always told me "Either you pay now or you pay later, but either way you are going to pay." It's just that simple.

Let's go back to Genesis 19:16. Lot lingered. He went to dragging. We tend to do that sometimes. We linger and drag because we're not really confident or sure that this is what God has for us. We do that sometimes when people come to us and encourage us to do this or that. When they follow up and ask, "Did you do it?" we say, "No, I haven't quite gotten there yet." We're lingering. We're dragging. We're not quite confident or sure that God has this for us. Otherwise, we would have done this long time ago.

> You must see your future and your destiny and make that your priority.

You must see your future and your destiny and make that your priority. Be urgent about this thing. If you're struggling with your finances, today is your day! You stop it! You don't linger with it anymore. If you're suffering within your body, within your relationship, or your finances, you say, "Today is the day. I am not dragging this along anymore. This is the day I cut loose my ball and chain!"

If you are ready to get out in the deep and set sail, then take command of your boat, pull that anchor up, and go full speed ahead. And that about settles that!

And we start new. I don't have to take yesterday into my today. If I do, guess what? If yesterday was bad, my today is already bad. That is why the scripture says not to go to sleep with anger upon your heart. You know why? Because you'll wake up with it. I have seen people where the minute that they wake up, it is already bad. "Uh, I guess I'll get up today." It's a blessing to get up today. You didn't wake yourself up. But since you went to bed so hot and so mad, I'm not speaking to you or anyone else today. Then your day is already messed up. I used to be that way. But I have the power to change it. "Hey I'm so sorry about yesterday; let's let that go." And that's all you have to do, just let it go. Sure I've made some bad financial mistakes. I've done this or I've done that. I'll let that go. But today I'm going to start saving a dollar. Today I'm going to start writing my budget down. Today I'm going to start saying some nice things to my wife. Today I'm going to start doing some nice things for my husband or children or family. Today I'm going to start focusing on what is in my heart to do. So I let yesterday go. Let it go. If you want to know how good your tomorrow is going to be, tell me what you're doing today. You set forth that in motion. It is connected. So we know that Lot lingered in verse 15.

In verse 16, we're talking about Lot. We're still getting ready to go to the next level. Genesis 19:16 says, "When he hesitated, the men grasped his hand and the hands of his wife and of his two daughters and led them safely out of the city, for the LORD was merciful to them" (NIV). That applies to us. Have you ever been dragging on some things and never really got quite to a 100 percent of doing them and God sent people in your life and blessed you anyway? Rather it is your friend, spouse, parent, sibling, mentor, or even a stranger that takes you under their wing and guidance and led you to your anointed place, people who will make sure you are cared for when you are going through some difficult times. I can attest to this. Can you? Ravens were sent because you prayed to God to help you, and they came and ministered you to safety. Yet for some reason, for the most part, if you are true to yourself and really think about it, most of these people you have never seen or heard from since. Know this. There are three types of people God sends to you. They come for different purposes and times in your life. They are a reason, a season, and a lifetime.

1. The "reason" folks' time in your life seems to vary in my opinion. Sometimes it is long, and sometimes it is prayed for. If not, God sends the people to help you out. But realize they are problem connected, which means as long as the problem or scenario remains, they remain. When the problem leaves, they also leave. It is never a breakup or abrupt departure, but they just seem to fade or fly away. You lose connection with them simply because you are no longer connected to your reason anymore. Now if you seem to be a slow learner and continue to not pass your test in life and do the same thing over and over, then these individuals may stay a bit longer, but once the problem is resolved they are gone.

2. The "season" folks last for a specific amount of time. Just like the seasons in a year, they are all set and scheduled. The reasons God has given us the different seasons is because they represent the

changes in our lives. Remember, as we learned in the last chapter about change, it is the very essence of growth. When we reach this point God will send a certain individual or group of people to help develop as we continue to mature. These people come into our lives when we are not sure about heading to a new place or have arrived at a new place and need to learn more. This a stage where we all feel a bit incomplete, and they fill in the spaces for us. The "season" folks assist us in becoming well rounded and complete with this new growth. They too will fade, but we sometimes maintain a relationship with them because of the impact and contribution they have made for such a period of time. But keep in mind that a season is a certain amount of time.

3. The "lifetime" folks obviously outlast the rest. They will be with you the whole time. Maybe not so much in the trenches as the other two, but they are always in your corner and by your side. These people you trust, and you respect the relationship you have with them. You have a lot in common with this group, and some are even your personal friends. God sends this group to support you, to walk with you, and to coach you all the way through. You don't spend a lot of time with them or talk to them much, but there is an understanding that undergirds the entire friendship. They will always be there to take you by the hand. Who are these people in your life? Think about them, and thank God for them.

They all keep you in line and accountable in some way shape or form. They ask questions like, "Did you call and check on that job?" You reply, "No, I really haven't had time." So they make sure it gets done, or they even call. "Did you go ahead and do this or that?" they ask. Again, "No, I haven't," is your response.

The Bible says that the Lord is merciful. This means He spares us from the punishment we deserve. He also is a gracious God, and He gives us things we really don't deserve.

I have children like that. They didn't do exactly what I told them to do, but they tried their best. So I blessed them anyway. That is good news! We serve a God like that. We would tell kids to clean their room, take the trash out, and wash the dishes, and then we would reward them. They took the trash out, kind of half-way washed the dishes, and threw some stuff in the closet, but you love them so much that you're going to give it to them anyway. That's mercy.

Mercy, in essence, is giving you things that you really don't deserve. I know I've gotten plenty of things in my life that I didn't quite deserve. Maybe you have also. Maybe you've gotten some things that made you say, "Lord, I don't know why You've done these things for me, but I thank You anyway." The Bible speaks of the angels taking the hand of Lot, his wife, and his children because of God's mercy. He blessed him anyway. (See Genesis 19:16.)

Yes, the man was dragging. We do that sometimes. We should have made it urgent within our business of handling something, but we didn't. God says, "I'm going to give it to them anyway." Example: You say, "I don't know why I'm going to go over and check on buying this house, because I know I can't afford it." And when you get in there the people tell you that you have been approved. Same thing. "I don't know why I'm applying for this job, because I know I really don't have all of the credentials and qualifications for it". They hire you anyway. Same thing. That is the type of merciful grace and loving God we serve. That can be exciting within itself. Even if I'm not quite there, God is going to bless me anyway. That's just the kind of God He is!

God's grace and goodness are not based on us. He can bless whomever He wants to bless. Sometimes we do that. Sometimes we see some not-so-righteous people getting blessed, and sometimes we have a problem with that. I cannot understand why they have all of that and they don't do right; they don't even praise Him! In fact, they don't do anything!

God says, "That's My love that you don't understand yet. In your eyes, they don't deserve it, and I didn't say that they did, but My love is so strong." That's the God we serve! That's the God that gets us excited. That's the God who is the reason why we sing. So it says that the Lord was merciful to them.

Genesis 19:17 (NIV) says:

> As soon as they had brought them out, one of them said, "Flee for your lives! Don't look back, and don't stop anywhere in the plain! Flee to the mountains or you will be swept away!"

"As soon as they had brought them out." Just think about that. The God that we serve is a Deliverer. He was preparing to smite Sodom and Gomorrah. He says, "Things are getting ready to happen in peoples' lives. The company is getting ready to shut down. People are about to get laid off. Things are about to get really hectic. Before they do, I'm going to bring you out. I'm going to bring you out because the enemy knows things are about to go wrong, and he wants you to get caught up in that. If you get caught up in that, then you lose focus and get distracted by him. That is what the enemy wants."

So the Lord will bring you out of whatever situation you are in, but you have to lean on Him. You have to move with Him. Notice He took them by the hand. Remember, that old saying, "Lord, take my hand. Lead me on"? Are you willing to follow Him when He takes your hand? Or are you going to hold back like a kid in the candy store when the parent says, "Come on, it's time to go"? The child wants to break down and act up, not knowing that the parent already has something for him.

You need to definitely understand that God will lead you out of your situation. You just need to simply have faith in Him, because there is nothing too big for the God we serve! We have a BIG God. Have you ever noticed that the God we serve is so big that He doesn't deal with little problems? I'll be honest with you. Think about it in your life. When the problems are little, He doesn't fool with them. He waits until a problem gets big. He says, "I want to see if you trust Me enough." You say, "Well, it's little right now." He says, "I know it." You ask, "Why didn't You come earlier?" He says, "I was waiting for it to get big." There are three reasons He was waiting for it to get big.

> You need to definitely understand that God will lead you out of your situation.

1. I've never seen a big God do little things. He would be out of character.

2. He's building your strength and faith to see whether you will let go of His hand or hold on.

3. The Father we serve likes a crowd. He doesn't mind folks at work talking about you. He doesn't mind family members whispering about your business or friends gossiping about you.

You know they're not going to make it. You know they're about to lose everything. I heard that their job is about to close. He says, "Fine, you let them say all of that. I'm going to use that. I'm going to let it get big enough so that they can count you out, and then I'm going to bring you out of it." That's the God we serve. He says, "Is it big enough? Now I'll step in. Just when they thought you were knocked out and counted out, I'm in now. I'm in now."

It's kind of like an insurance deductible. We all have deductibles. If the problem isn't big enough for the deductible, the insurance tells you to handle it. It's only when it gets big enough that they step in. If you have a $1,000 deductible, and only $900 worth of damage, you deal with it. Anytime it gets over a $1,000, they step in.

That's the God we serve. It's just that simple and that plain. Don't panic about it. You must be assured that you're assured within the Word of God. He will deliver you out of your situations.

God told Lot and his family to flee for your lives. You must run for your destiny and your future as if today were the last day. God was getting ready to wipe out this entire city. He was telling them to get out and run as fast as they could from this situation.

Do we still hang around our situations? I'm supposed to be a recovering alcoholic, but I'm still hanging around people who drink. I better run from those guys as soon as I can. I am trying to strengthen my marriage, but I'm still living wrong. I need to run from her, as far as I can. And then God goes on to say, "Don't look back!"

This is very important. How can I possibly step into my future when I'm stuck in my past? I have to let them go. A lot of guys I used to run with when I was single, I had to move on when I got married. It's not a matter of me disconnecting with them or thinking I'm better than them. But I'm running toward my future, and my future is to stay married with my wife forever. I can't look back now. I run across guys who are now married, who've been married, who want to stay married, and that's in my future.

I can't look back. So, I messed up at this job, but at my next job that's not going to happen. So I did something wrong back there, but I won't do that again. And it changes. God said if you're going to go to the next level, "Don't look back." That is a command. Don't do it. Now the people who don't want to see you go to the next level will bring up your history. "Well, you know you've done this. Well, you know you've done that." And that's fine; you acknowledge it and say, "Yes, but that was my past, and let's leave the past in the past." We serve a God who says, "Do not look back!" Flee to the mountains. The mountain is the highest peak there is. He says run to the top. What is it that you are trying to do? What is it you want to do? What is it you want to be? GO FOR IT!

I am reminded of Colonel Sanders, the KFC guy. Before he started creating his recipe for chicken, he was well beyond retirement age. The colonel looked at his situation and said, "This is not going to do it." There are things that you look at in your life and say, "This is not enough. I'm not taking it. I'm going to run to the mountains." The mountain is the top.

What is it you want? Or are you just willing to settle for what's given to you? No matter how you look at it, you made a choice. If you did something about it or you didn't do anything, you made a choice. Run to the mountains. Run to the very top. Become partners with people who are trying to go that way.

Get with people who are going where you desire to be. It is so true that birds of a feather flock together. Who are you running with? My grandmother always told me, "Show me three of your friends, and I will tell you all about you." I don't care if it's Crazy Joe; there is something within you that connects with Crazy Joe. I don't care if you run with Larry, Mo, and Curly; they all act differently, but they are within you. You just know how to cover yours up. There is something that you like about each one of them that is within you. The scripture says, "Flee to the mountains, to the top, or you will be swept away."

What does "you'll be swept away" mean? It means He is about to destroy Sodom and Gomorrah. He is about ready to wipe out this particular area if you don't flee to the top. Run for the best in your marriage, run for your best in finances, run for your best in health. Otherwise, whatever He's trying to take you away from will only consume you. That'll be your punishment.

Most people don't get out of their situation because they can't let that situation go. I have a relative who went into the military. Great choice. I'll tell anyone that the military is a great institution. Well the thing is, my relative came home every weekend. He never got away. He came back to the exact same thing that he left. But the people who got away didn't come back to the same situation. You went, but you didn't go back. I went, but I didn't go back. It was a blessing from God to just get away from all of the bad elements.

You need to run to the hills or to the mountains. But they can't because they're caught up in a situation. It's just that simple. We all grow up with these practical sayings: "You can take the cow out of the country, but you can't take the country out of the cow." You have to get from around these people if you want to go to the next level. If you're making Cs and Ds in your life, you better get around some A students. There is a good chance that you will at least move to a B, if not an A. But you can forget about As if you're hanging around Cs and Ds. Quit trying to change those people. They like it just the way it is. Believe it or not, those people don't want As and Bs. And when you start making As and Bs, they're not inspired; they want you to fall right back to the Cs and Ds.

Some might be saying, "Yeah, he thinks he's something since his life is going well, but he'll be back." But I won't be back as long as I stay away from them. "You don't come around anymore." Well, why do you think I'm staying on top? That's fine. I'm talking about friends and family. Those are the main people who will choke the life out of you. Jesus says it best. He says, "The weeds choke the life out of the plants." What is "choking your life"? Bringing those things up. Bringing the past up. You're just trying to kill me. You're just trying to hurt me because you see no vision, no mountains in your life.

That's what real jealousy is. A guy who is already rich

doesn't mind talking to another rich guy. But a poor guy hates to see a rich guy. But that's a fool. Now, a guy who has a good heart and desires to be rich looks forward to a rich guy coming by. Now that's wisdom! "Hey friend, how are you doing? I can learn something from you. I just need to figure out how you did what you did to get what you have." I know my God is no respecter of persons, because whatever worked for you should be able to work for me. But it won't work for a fool, because he can't understand. He hates it. Unfortunately, we may have many fools in our own families.

That is why I pray that each and every household, each and every family has one or two that get to the mountain. Then, you will be able to see a whole lot of things more clearly up there. Now you can go back in the valley and get the others. It won't be everybody, but there will be two or three who will say, "I believe now. You did it, and now I know it can be done." But if that person had never gotten away to the mountains, that would have never happened. In most families people say, "We don't have any successful relatives." That's because you're killing them! When someone speaks positively about starting their own business or doing something, you talk them out of it. I listen to other positive people with businesses, and the first thing they do with their children is figure out how they can put them in the business, or a business. They try to get them to the mountain. They don't want to leave anyone in the valley. But when we start talking about the mountains, all of the people in the valley get mad: "You think you're better than us."

The others say, "I need you to get to the mountains, and whatever I can do to get you there, I will. Why? Because that is how I can get out! That's a wise person. That's how I get out, by helping you get there. In that situation, everybody wins. But you can't say that to a loser because he has no vision. So we must flee from these people. We must run to the mountains and not look back, or we will be swept away.

Genesis 19:18–19 (NIV) says:

> But Lot said to them, "No, my lords, please! Your servant has found favor in your eyes, and you have shown great kindness to me in sparing my life. But I can't flee to the mountains; this disaster will overtake me, and I'll die."

God told him to flee to the mountains. There is a gift, a calling that God has placed in every human being. What do we say? What did Lot say: "I can't." He said it, but the Lord told him he could do it. The Lord says, "I'll see you at the top," and you say, "I can't get to the top." Suppose someone is making $5 an hour, and the Lord tells him that he's going to make $25 an hour; the person replies, "I can't do that." Jesus replies, "How long have I been with you? Have I been wasting my time with you?" That's what He told the disciples in John 14. Isn't that what we tell our kids? You can do this, or you can do that, and then they say, "I don't know about that, Mom. I don't know about that, Dad. I don't think or believe that I can do that." Sure, you can make it. Who says you can't?

If God says it, it's done. But I guess that's the enemy within us telling us that. You have been hanging in the valley, hanging in the lows too long. Notice now, that this is the same Lot who was with Abraham (a blessed and godly man, a righteous man, and a friend of God). Notice that

Abraham wasn't there. When Lot was with Abraham, wherever Abraham said, "Let's go," Lot went.

That's why it is so important and good to be around people who have vision, who are connected with God, and who are at the mountain. Now, if I'm debt free and you're hanging around me, that is all you talk about now. "I know I'm coming out of this." If I have a good marriage and you're trying to have a good marriage, you begin to know that you can have a good marriage. But instead, we hang around the opposite people.

Notice that Lot doesn't have Abraham anymore. He's by himself. He says, "I can't do it." If he were with his uncle Abraham, he would have never said that because Abraham knows that God told him, "I am your great rewarder." There is nothing you can't do, because God is with you. He says, "Lord, I know You have favor on me, for sparing my life and for taking me to the next level and not letting this relationship or this alcohol, or my depression, or my finances or all these bad thoughts kill me. I appreciate it. But I don't think I can make it to that place You're talking about. That's too big for me. I don't think I can have that."

God says that you can have that $100,000 or $200,000 house, and you say, "I can't have that, just give me a nice little house that's all right for me." God says, "Go to the mountains"; Lot says, "I can't do that because that's too big for me. I can't afford that. That might kill me." We know that whatever God gives to you, he adds no sorrow to it. Don't sweat it. Don't worry about it. If God gave it to you, He'll provide it. If the parents move into a big house, do you think the kids are asking about how much the mortgage is? No, they could care less. If Daddy says we can have it, then we have it. That's how it works. That's how it is. That's the God we serve!

Today you can start anew by not telling Him that "I can't," but instead telling Him that "I WILL! I am whatever You say I am. I can be whatever You say I can be. I can do whatever You say I can do. I can have whatever You say I can have." Are we searching? Are we seeking? Are we fleeing to the mountains? That's the top. God desires for us all to be at the top. Or have you countered Him and told Him that you just can't do it?

Today you can start anew by not telling Him that "I can't," but instead telling Him that "I WILL!"

Genesis 19:20 says, "Look, here is a town near enough to run to and it is small" (NIV). I want you to get this because this is Lot talking to God. How many times have we said this same thing? He says, "Look, there is a town near here. Let me flee to that town. It is very small isn't it? And then my life will be spared." I know you're saying the same thing that I said. Lot has talked himself out of something great that God was about to give him. God says to the person who has no car, "You can have a Mercedes or a Lexus." But that person says, "You can just give me a Pinto and I'll be all right." You're in a one-bedroom apartment, and God says that you can have a four-bedroom house with a two- or three-car garage. And you say, "No, a two-bedroom apartment will be enough for me." You're making $5 an hour, and God says that you can make $30 an hour. You say, "If You just give me $6.50, that'll be enough for me." Did he not talk himself out of it?

The mountains are too big for me. I can't see myself having that. I can't see myself owning my own business. I can't see myself having a good marriage. I can't see myself debt free. I can't see myself being physically healthy in my body, going to the gym working out, walking every day, and eating right. Mountains are too hard for me. Just remove this little pain in my knee and I'll be all right.

God says, "You don't know Me at all." He has talked himself out of it. It's like I'm about to give my son $100, and he says "No, Daddy, if you just give me $3, that will be good." That is what Lot did.

Do we not do that? We all must take an inventory of ourselves. Have we really talked ourselves out of stuff?

Oh, I know I'm guilty. Before I came to realize who He is, what He has, and who I am, I told Him, "If you do this, that's good enough for me." He says, "Oh no, don't say that. Just tell Me to do it and you stay out of it." How about that, just get out of the way. That is why he told Lot to flee. Get out of the way, so that I can do this. This is enough for me. If you say the mountains are mine, then I'm going to run. Paul said, "I'm going to run the race. I fought the good fight, so that I may receive my prize." (See 2 Timothy 4:7–8.) If He says it's there, then I'm going for it. Whoever is running with me, get to running. Anyone who is not running with me, well, they are going to talk about me anyway. That's why I'm not looking back, because I don't care who's talking about me. They'll see it when I get my prize. And there are a few of them who are going to want to run with me after they see I've received my prize. God says, "I'm going to use your life as a testimony, as a witness, to get the people that I want out."

Before the angels came to Sodom and Gomorrah, God came to find the people He wanted to get out. They didn't believe. You have to believe God. If He spoke to your heart and said the mountains are yours, I suggest you run to it because it's already blessed. It's already anointed. It is actually waiting on you. There are some of us that our destinies have been waiting, saying that he should've been showing up right about now, but I don't see him. You've stopped running. That marriage should be right by now, but they stopped running. How about this one? "Lord, if you could just help me make it through the day."

Is that it? Is that all you want? We have to be careful about the things we say.

People say if you have a job that should be enough. No, I hear they have management positions; why can't I have that? Be careful of the people in the valley. That is why Lot needed someone to run with. When he was with his uncle Abraham, a friend of God, he was blessed. As a matter of fact, the only reason he was able to get out of Sodom is because his uncle prayed for him. God said, "I'm going to wipe out everybody," but Uncle Abraham asked, "What if you find a few righteous in there?" He thought about his nephew.

How many people have prayed for you that you don't even know about? How many people don't even know that you prayed for them? Abraham said, "My nephew lives there. You're not going to kill everybody, are you?" God said, "No, I wouldn't do that." How many people do you know who are at a job that you heard was going to have a lay off? You realize your sister works there, and you start praying. A big hurricane hits the coast, and you think about your family members who live there. Right then and there you start praying for them. That's what saves them.

Prayer changes things. God answers prayers. If I see a car accident during my prayer time, and one of the cars looks like the car of someone I know, I pray right then because God hears them. That's the reason Lot was spared. A friend of God, a righteous man, prayed for Lot.

Don't talk yourself out of your blessings! If you have to run with a new crowd, I suggest you get to running, and don't look back. Otherwise, you'll be swept away from the situation you're already in. Don't look back; it will cost you. I know couples who have been married ten years, fifteen, twenty, twenty-five, thirty, forty years, fifty years, fight for sixty years. Fight for seventy. People say it gets easier, but says who? Oh, if you're making this much money, you have it made. Says who? I have more bills, too. I'm fighting for this. I'm fleeing to the mountains. I'm fleeing to the best of what God has spoken for my life. Whatever He has spoken into your life today, claim it. Receive it. Your day is today!

Many of life's failures are people who did not realize how close they were to success when they gave up.
—Thomas Jefferson

Through tough times character is not built, but revealed.
—Unknown

You don't have to worry about breaking God's promises if you stand on them.
—Unknown

When there's no insight, do not expect an outcome.
—Ellis Powell

Whoever seeks to save his life will lose it, and whoever loses his life will preserve it.
—Luke 17:33, NKJV

Seven

LET IT GO

LETTING GO IS so difficult for a lot of people for many different reasons. For some, it is because of past failures or past mistakes. For others, it has to do with forgiveness, either with someone else or even themselves. It may be a business that failed, mistakes that cost a job, bad judgment, or reactions that broke a relationship. As we look back at Lot's story, let's learn from his ordeal. He had told God that he'd rather go to a small town. Now God told him to head for the mountains, head for the top. That's a good father. "Son, don't cut yourself short, head to the mountaintop." But instead he said, "No, I don't believe I can make it." I don't believe I can be a millionaire. I just don't believe that I can get my degree. I just don't believe I can really make $30 per hour when I'm making $5 now. I just don't believe that I can have a good marriage right now. I don't really believe

121

I can have that. So just give me a little something. That's what he told God. I really don't believe that I can make it to the mountain.

Let's go to Genesis 19:21.

> And he said to him, "See, I have favored you concerning this thing also, in that I will not overthrow this city for which you have spoken."

God said to him, "If this is all you want for your life, fine, I'll do it." Notice, though, that isn't what he told him. God told him, "You can be this. You can do this. You can have this." Lot said, "No, God."

I know Lot isn't the only one who has made some crazy requests like that. Because we can't see that far, we can't see through God's eyes. Lord, if you'll just get me out of this, that'll be just enough. I can attest and say that Lot isn't by himself, because I know I've been guilty of saying those same types of things. "If You'll just do this, that's enough," not realizing I am cutting myself off from the best God has for me. Since you can't see what I have for you in your life—whether it's finishing school, a larger house, a happy marriage, or promotion to management—since you can't see My way, I'll give you what you asked for."

An old wise saying goes, "Be careful what you ask for, because you just might get it." So now I've just learned to say, "God, just do Your will," because I know His will is bigger than my little request. God's will is perfect and blessed. We also know that God can do more than we can hope or imagine. So, I'm not going to put in my little two cents. "God, just leave my stuff out and do what You were going to do, because I know that You're able and capable and willing to do it all."

He told Lot to head for the mountain. You know, something stirs in your spirit and says, "I know you just started this $5 per hour job, but go ahead and apply for management." What do we do? Talk ourselves out of it. "They're not going to hire me. They're not going to give me this. I don't have enough experience. I don't think I can do that." I'm not the only one who has said that to myself. "I don't think I can be debt free. I don't think I can become that. God, just help me pay off my one charge card and I'll be all right."

He said to Lot, "See, I have favored you." There is nothing better than God's favor upon your life, for it is better than silver and gold. There is nothing like a child having the favor of his own father. That means your request is good to go. What is it you want? Don't hide your thoughts and desires because God says He'll give you the desires of your heart. Don't make a little request that you don't have a car and you're thinking, *If I could just get a Ford, I'll be all right.* God says, "What do you want? I've favored you." What is it? Go ahead and throw in the best right now. You have favor. This is your anointed and appointed time. This is your season. What do you want? Every time Jesus was ministering, He would ask, "What do you want from Me?"

God's favor is right now. Most people have not understood the seasons for their life. I believe everyone has a season and a time, just like every animal and plant—a time to change, to grow, to increase, and to multiply. Scripture states that there is a time and a season for *everything* (Eccles. 3). Believe it or not, that includes you, too!

What is it you want from God right now? This is your time, your season, your year of favor. What is it you want?

I dare you to say, "Just give me this little bit right here." Remember, He'll say, "All right, if that's all you want, fine." I'll take a few hundred or a few thousand. Or if you could just get this old part of my body working I'll be fine. Heal my whole body. Make me feel like I'm twenty years younger. If I can get anything I want, I may as well go for the top. I may as well head for the mountains. If your marriage is struggling, don't say, "Lord, if we can just stop arguing, that's fine with me." No, I want to go for the best. She can be my best friend again! He can be my best friend again! We can talk again. We can laugh again. We can go places again. We can enjoy life again. Remind me why we got married and the love we had. If I can make any request, I may as well go for it all.

Nothing is too hard or impossible for God. I've been in *my* way long enough, messing up things. So I'll get out and let God in. Lot had favor, and he should have made his request known right then. But notice, God said, "Concerning this thing also, in that I will not overthrow this city for which you have spoken" (Gen. 19:21). Since Lot said, "I would rather go here; there are some jobs, communities, and families," God said, "I won't do anything to them because now you're in it." He was going to overthrow it. That city was as good as destroyed. But since the favor of God was on Lot, and wherever he went, God blessed.

Some companies or businesses would have been shut down a long time ago if there weren't saints and righteous people of God on board. Neighborhoods would have already been treacherous and vandalized, but saints live in that place. God says, "I'm not going to overthrow it."

Let me refresh your memory and go back a little bit.

Before God initiated the destruction of Sodom and Gomorrah, He went to Abraham. Abraham's last request was, "If
You find ten righteous, will You not save it all?" If there were
ten people there, God would have saved the cities. People
tend to think it was all about homosexuality, and that was
part of it. The main reason was because the hearts of the
people were bad, wicked, and evil. That's what it boils down
to. If there were ten people there, God would have saved the
region. It's not about how much bad was in there. It boils
down to how many God-fearing people were there. That is
the only thing that is saving corporation, cities, states, and
countries. There are just enough righteous people in it. That
is what saves the multitudes.

The fact that Lot went to that town is what saved that
town. Now that was Lot's request, not God's. God told him
to go to the mountains. But Lot said, "I would rather go to
this little town nearby." God said, "Go to the mountains.
Get far away from here. I'm about to take you to the next
level. I need you to get away from these people saying these
old things, thinking these old thoughts, going to these old
places." We say, "I really don't want to go that far away from
them. I am really comfortable."

God says, "I'm trying to promote you," and you say, "But
I don't want to leave them because they're my party buddies…my drinking buddies…my smoking buddies…my
high school buddies. I don't want to go that far." That's what
God is saying in Genesis 19:21. "All right, I have something
for you, but since you can't seem to tear yourself away from
them, it's not a problem." God said, "Hurry, escape there,
for I cannot do anything until you arrive there."

The name of the city Lot went to was called Zoar. If

you recall, Lot said, "Please let me escape there (is it not a little one)?" (Gen. 19:20). Lot named the city. He in essence spoke his future. He said, "Is this not a little town. Is this not a little place for me?" God had a BIG place for him. But Lot couldn't see himself having that, so he said, "I'll just take this little place." He called and spoke that into existence. What is it that you called into existence? Your little town. Your little future. Your small harvest. Stop worrying about people talking about you because they are going to do that anyway.

If God placed this on your heart, stay around and be around people who will continue to influence you, build your confidence, and tell you to receive what God has promised you. "Well, if you could say that God told you to be a millionaire, but your family might say that nobody told you that," then you're hanging around the wrong people. I told you to let it go. "If you would say that God told me I was going to be debt free, but if you say that around your friends who are in debt," they're going to say, "Get out of here. My friends are going to say things about me." You need to let them go. If you are going to reach a place in your life you have never been, then you must be willing to ignore some things and some people. Lot didn't really want to let them go. God told him to get far away from here, but Lot asked to just go to the next neighborhood. He didn't want to get too far from them.

> If you are going to reach a place in your life you have never been, then you must be willing to ignore some things and some people.

How many of you are just realizing that you need to let some things go? Solomon has said in the Scriptures, "There is a time for everything" (Eccles 3:1). I love one particular thing he says also: There is a time to keep and there is a time to throw away (Eccles 3:6, NIV). How many things have we just been holding on to? How many people have we just been holding on to? How many old places have we just been holding on to? These things are delaying us from reaching our destiny. LET IT GO! LET IT GO! Genesis 19:23–24 says, "The sun had risen upon the earth when Lot entered Zoar. Then the LORD rained brimstone and fire on Sodom and Gomorrah, from the LORD out of the heavens."

So God overthrew those cities, all the plains, all the inhabitants of the cities, and what grew on the ground. He destroyed all of the cities, all of plains, all of the people, and all of the ground. God wiped everything out. He cleaned house. How many of our houses need to be cleaned? I do it twice a year, personally. Every six months I go through my whole house, from the bedroom to the kitchen to the garage. Anything that is not serving its purpose must go.

Most people have nice houses, but they are junky. Most marriages are junky, with extra stuff and baggage. How many times have you passed by someone's house and their garage looks like a storage room? Get rid of that stuff and bless someone else with it. Do a spring-cleaning in your life by letting go of things. What am I doing with two can openers? Two toasters? Something needs to go. Some of that can be used to bless someone else. But some people hold on to it. Now if what I have in my hand is enough, I'm going to hold on to it. But if what you have in your hand isn't enough, I suggest you let it go. That's the only way you're going to receive something else. It's creating room for a new place. You have to do some spring-cleaning in your life. You're the temple that God lives in. Clean your house up. Clean up your marriage. Clean up your relationships with your kids. Clean up your habits. Stop spending more money than you actually make and saying things that you really don't mean.

Lot called it, spoke it, and there it was. Stop saying things because you're mad. You're tearing your own house down. You're cluttering your life with problems, sorrow, issues, and grief. You talk about it and say that Satan is bringing all the problems. Are you sure? To me it sounds like you are doing a pretty good job of it. The enemy is really In-Me. He is never too far. Just go look in the mirror; there is at times your biggest opposition. Stop calling her names. Stop calling him names. Why are you tearing your house down and then saying, "Well, I'm sorry"?

Let me share a story with you. There was a father who had a little boy that was five years old. He told the little boy to put a nail in the fence every time he said something hurting to another individual. By the end of the school week, the boy had thirty nails in the fence. Then his father made him think about what he did and then apologize to all of those people he had said hurting things to. After he had apologized to them, the boy was to remove all the nails from the fence. He pulled every nail out of the fence. The father then asked the son, "Did you understand what I had you do?" The son replied, "Yes, I did everything you told me, but for some reason, there are holes in the fence." The holes in the fence are what weakens it if we don't patch things up again, which allows anyone to come through.

And that's what happens when we leave holes in our relationships, finances, or situations that allow Satan to come through. Satan sees that since we've knocked holes in it, he may as well go ahead and tear the rest of it down. Why do we do that? I've heard one great quote that says, "Sometimes saying nothing is the best thing to say." It's OK if she made you mad. It's OK if he made you mad. Take it to God. Pray for them. I remember when a bully tried to pick on me and I said, "I'm going to tell my daddy on you." He wanted to know, "Why do you have to go get your daddy?" Because you know I'm going to get someone of higher authority who can take care of you. I don't have time to fight with you. I don't have time to argue with you. You just want to start something, because something wicked and evil has stirred within you. But I'm not going to tear my house down. That is the same house I have to live in. We've knocked holes all in the roof, and we wonder why our relationship is leaky. Don't do that. Clean your house out. An old saying goes, "Don't worry about sweeping around somebody else's house. Sweep around your own house."

I don't know if you've noticed this, but dust builds up in any house (big, small, valuable, or cheap). But, did you know that most of the dust in your house actually comes from the dirt you bring in? We are the ones complaining about dusting the house, when really I am the one polluting my own house. If you've been to anybody's house visiting, and you see how dusty it is, look at the individual. How they take care of their house is probably how they take care of their finances, their relationships, and their relationship with God. All of that comes from within. If dust has built up, they're not tending to it. It takes a lot to continue dusting every week. You have to develop, practice, and make it a habit; then it becomes natural. We have to make it a practice and habit to clean our house.

So God overthrew everything in Genesis 19:25. He overthrew those cities, all the plains, all of the inhabitants, and everything on the ground. It was all bad. Remember in 1 Samuel, God told Saul to go in that town and kill everything. Saul said, "Why everything? Do you mean the babies, too?" And God said, "Yes, because it is the adults who will corrupt those same kids. It's just a matter of time before little Johnny is going to be just like his daddy. It's just a matter of time, so get him now and you don't have to worry about him."

So God wiped out everything. How many of us have not taken heed to the word of God and are seeing things wiped out? He has warned you, but you haven't taken heed. And then we wonder why we're struggling. He said go, escape for your life and don't look back. When you're struggling through your marriage or your finances, cut some of those things loose. You can't continue to try and have a good marriage when you're still hanging around friends who are still going out drinking, smoking, and all of that kind of bad stuff. You can't compete with that. You had better run to the mountains quick.

Genesis 19:26 states, "But…(*but* is big, I mean this *BUT* is big).

Johnny says, "Mom, can I go outside?" Mom says, "Yes, you can go outside, but…" Anything after *but* is more powerful than what was said before. "You can, but if you do this, it negates everything else that I said." *But* is BIG. I mean I love you and all, BUT…That means forget all that I love you because it's gone. The *but* is what supersedes everything. We can do this, BUT...I wouldn't normally say this, BUT...So forget all that I said earlier, because this is where the rubber meets the road, so to speak. BUT is contingent on you doing whatever follows. That means this is about to change everything.

Verse 26 states, "But his wife looked back." This is very important. This is his family going with him into this place. They have made it in this place. Remember, God cannot do anything until everyone has made it in the town. She cannot move forward because she is not willing to let go of the past. How hard is it to have a good marriage when you have a husband or wife who keeps looking back? We're married now (you're not single now), stop looking back! You don't do this anymore. You don't say this anymore. You don't go here anymore. You have to let it go!

There comes a special moment in everyone's life, a moment for which that person was born. When he seizes it, it is his finest hour.

—Winston Churchill

If you are able to see it, then seize it, because it just a matter of time as you believe it, you'll start to achieve it and ultimately receive it.

—Ellis Powell

He who observes the wind will not sow, and he who regards the clouds will not reap.

—Ecclesiastes 11:4, NKJV

For everyone who asks receives, and he who seeks finds, and to him who knocks it will be opened.

—Luke 11:10, NKJV

And let us not grow weary while doing good, for in due season we shall reap if we do not lose heart.

—Galatians 6:9, NKJV

Eight

SEIZE THE MOMENT

L ET ME START this chapter with a quotation: "Making the Best." My business is not to remake myself, but to make the absolute best of what God made. My business is not to remake myself; people are always trying to change themselves. Why are you trying to change? Thank God the birds are not trying to be snakes, and the snakes are not trying to be fish, and the fish are not trying to be cats, and cats aren't trying to be dogs. Be the best He made you, and that's all. Don't try to be Suzie or Bobby or Jimmy. Be the best you! There are some things I need to work on in order for me to be the best me, but I don't need me to try to be the best you and vice versa.

> My business is not to remake myself, but to make the absolute best of what God made.

Never forget if you want to know more about you; ask God to reveal it to you. It all starts with God. If you want to know what a Ford Expedition or Ford Explorer does, check with Ford. If you want to know what the creation does, check with the creator. If you want to know what an invention does, check with the inventor. So this is where it starts.

A tree never stops going to the next level, for if it did, it would start dying. Believe it or not, it is always growing. Even when you can't see at the top, it is strengthening its roots underneath the surface. Also when the seasons change, it continues to change. So it is always going to the next level. So, we are in the next chapter called "Seize the Moment." When God speaks to you, do you seize the moment? Seize means to take possession, to take hold of quickly, to take prisoner. When God speaks to you, do you seize it? Do you take it prisoner? Do you arrest it? Do you take His Word and detain it? When people get arrested, they go downtown to whatever jail station they're taken to and put in a cell, and they don't leave.

When you hold His Word hostage, it can only be released when God has manifested that which He said He spoke in your life. You have to seize it, to take possession of it. When I look at the word *possession*, possession is simply property. So God's Word is property. He says it's mine, but I am going to give it to you.

To seize the moment. *Moment* is defined as just a brief interval in time. Notice, it's a *brief* interval. It's a particular point in time, a time of excellence and importance. So when God speaks, God is speaking into your life for a brief interval. He is speaking into your life at a particular point in time, and this point in time is of importance and excellence.

Some of us miss it because we don't seize it.

I've never seen getting ready to go to the next level dealing with Lot at all until God had opened His insight to me. We know that in verse 26, Lot's wife looked back, and you can't go to the next level looking back. We've talked about that and about forgetting the former things and looking forward to a new thing. That's what we should be doing, looking forward to a new thing.

Whatever we messed up on yesterday, that was yesterday. Today is a new day. God asked through the prophet Isaiah, "Do you not perceive this new thing I'm doing? This new thing is a new day." (See Isaiah 43:19.) That's it. Now get in it and manifest and seize the moment. Genesis 19:27 reads, "And Abraham went early in the morning to the place where he had stood before the LORD." Unlike Lot, Abraham understood God and had a closer relationship with Him.

Remember now, Abraham is the one who asked God to save Lot and his family. Abraham is the one who actually asked God to save the whole town: "Lord, if You find at least ten, would You not save them all?" And God said, "Yes, I will." So you have a righteous man, a God-fearing man, a friend of God, asking God to not only save his family but also everybody else. Are we faithful people like Abraham, not only praying for our families, but also for everyone else?

Not only do I pray for my son at school, I also pray for his teachers and his school because it's all connected to him. And if it's connected to him, and he is connected to me, then they are, too. Again, I am just trying to show you the righteousness of this man Abraham. He prayed not only for his family but also for all of Sodom and Gomorrah. Had

God found ten righteous, He would have saved everybody. He would have spared them. So we must learn from this.

Notice that Abraham went early in the morning. Have you ever just gotten up early in the morning? He got up "early." Scripture could have just said that Abraham got up in the morning, which meant just any old typical morning. But not this particular morning, because yesterday Abraham had an encounter with God.

When was the last time you had an encounter with God? When was the last time that God sent someone in your life that spoke to you, and the next day you rose early? You rose early because that word was in your spirit. Or did you just go back to sleep and wake up at the normal time that you usually wake up? *Are you seizing the moment?* Abraham woke up early. Remember now, it was just the day before that he had talked with God about saving Lot and his family. God had already spoken to him.

How many of us have been spoken to by God and we have yet to get up early? I don't know about you, but when people get up early, that kind of shows me that there is a sign of anticipation. There is a sign of expectation. It's like the kids at Christmas. They get up early for some reason. The first day of school—they get up early for some reason. On Saturdays, they seem to get up early for some reason. There is anticipation. There is expectation. Abraham got up early because he was expecting God to do what He said. That is the only reason he got up early. Because I spoke with my God and I know He is going to do exactly what He said.

Abraham said, "If God said it, I had better get up early and start to receive it. I'm going to set my clock early." You know that old saying, "The early bird gets the worm." He's seizing his moment. I'm going to hold to it until I can see that God has brought what He said to pass. That is the only reason he got up early.

What has God spoken to us in our lives, and we have yet to get up early to see if God has done what He said? "And Abraham went early in the morning, to the place where he had stood before the LORD." He went back to the place that he received his word. There are many of us that God has spoken in our lives, yesterday, last week, last month, last year, ten years, or even twenty years ago. Are you going back to that place in your mind where you said, "Yes, I knew that God had spoken to me. Yet I did not seize the moment." Think about it. Is there something that comes to your mind that you know God spoke to you about and you didn't do anything about it? I have had those times, too. But not anymore, because today we're learning how to seize the moment. It's right here. That's the place he went back to.

Whatever promises God made to you, go back there and bring those things to remembrance. The reason he walked all the way back to that place is because that place caused him to remember what God said. Go back to yesterday. Go back last month. Go back last year. Go back until you say, "Yes, Lord, You promised me this." And God will say, "I just wanted to see if you would go back to the place I told you." It's not that hard.

How many of us have received the Word and have not taken a stand? God has spoken to your life and said you should do this. You should have this. You can be this, but you have yet to take a stand.

When are you going to take a stand? You know you

should be this. You know you should be there. You know you should do this, but yet you have not taken a stand. You're almost finished with school, but you won't go back. God has spoken to you, but you won't go back. You know you should strive for better, but you won't. You have yet to take a stand. You've accepted mediocrity. Or do you do what Lot did, choose your own path? I don't want to go there, I'll go there instead. I'll do that *later*. You had better seize the moment.

Let me be honest with you: it's not as if you're going back and forward talking to God every day. So when He speaks, surely there should be urgency. I mean I have a computer, and I get e-mails. I don't get e-mails all of the time, but when that thing says, "You've got mail," I had better check it right then. It could be a message of importance.

When God speaks to you, you had better grab it and hold on tight. Take a stand right then. Or do you just choose not to worry about it? That will hinder you from getting to the next level. If you're struggling in your finances, seize the moment and take a stand. If you're struggling in your relationship, seize the moment and take a stand.

"If a man doesn't stand for something, he'll fall for anything."

If you're struggling in your career, seize the moment and take a stand. The old saying is, "If a man doesn't stand for something, he'll fall for anything." We're falling for all of the tricks of the devil, which continue to tell us we will fail. That day was his day.

Whatever you want, you can ask for it right now. Scripture says, "And whatever things you ask in prayer, believing, you will receive" (Matt. 21:22). Seize the moment! This is your time, but it is only for a brief time. That means that when the door opens, you had better run (like you know what) in there. When spring comes, you had better drop those seeds in the ground. Now is the time. Seize the moment. No one plants in the fall. You've missed your time. When God speaks to you, you had better do it right now! Nobody asked for you to understand it. Trust in Him and stand on Him.

I have kids. They don't understand everything I do. I'm just looking for obedience and for them to trust me. They'll see and I'll reveal to them after they've done it. After they've taken a stand and stood on my word. Anything I've told them, all they have to do is go back to the place and remember my word. And I will bring it to pass. If we go back to our place and take a stand, there is happiness there. There is healing there. When someone is able to speak into your life and you remember that they said they were going to do something for you, do you not feel that joy that comes within your life? Don't you start feeling all those things that you thought you should have had a long time ago?

Some of should have been way ahead a long time ago. Go back in your mind to when God spoke to you and seize that. People say, "If I could go back in time..." Sure you can. We just learned that time is just a moment. Go back in it. *Seize it!* Hold on to it, because His Word never changes, but it is everlasting. He is still there. You moved on. Go back to your place. What has God told you that you should be doing? Where has He told you that you should be? Say that I'm not going to give this up. I'm going to seize it. I'm going to hold it. I'm going to arrest it until He brings it to pass. Let me show you how He does that in a really practical sense.

Genesis 19:28 (NIV) says:

> He looked down toward Sodom and Gomorrah, toward
> all the land of the plain, and he saw dense smoke rising
> from the land, like smoke from a furnace.

He looked. First Abraham went back to the spot where God had given him His word. Then he looked at his life. He looked at the situation, and God had surely done what He said He would do.

That's what we must do! That's how we're able to see that God has taken us to the next level!

We must understand this. It's really practical and really down to earth. It says, "He looked down." If he were able to look down, that means he was up. No matter what the situation is that is going on in your life, God will always elevate you and cause you to rise above your situation. Abraham looked down. He looked down at Sodom and Gomorrah. Sodom and Gomorrah were in the valley. If he was able to look down in the valley, he had to be up in the mountains—the same place God told Lot to go. God had said, "Head for the mountains. Escape for your life." Lot didn't head to the mountains. Lot went to a nearby town, and a small town at that. God said you have favor and you can ask for whatever you want, because this is your moment! Lot picked a small town. I can live any place in the country and I'm going to choose a place with a population of thirty-five. I can have any job I want, and I'm going to choose a job making $5.50 per hour.

This is your time. If God is speaking to you, this is your moment. Seize it! The ground is fertile. Drop as many seeds as you want to in the ground. But we won't. If I can just get a tree out of the deal, I'll be all right. I have literally heard people brag about not having enough—as if that is going to get them any closer to heaven. God says, "Your time is now. You have favor now."

We even saw when Lot said, "I know I have favor from You, and thank You. But just give me this little bit." (See Genesis 19:21.) No, we're not doing that. If it's my moment, I want all that God has for me! Don't withhold anything from me! If this is my season, this is my time, this is my moment, and I want it all!

When we are struggling in all sorts of things, it is because we are not dwelling in the mountains. We are still struggling and fighting with people in the valley. That is why God told Lot to get away from all of this. You can't go to the next level dealing with the same people, dealing with the same thoughts, dealing and going to the same places. You just can't. Abraham understood that, and that is why he dwelled in the mountains. And he saw. Abraham looked down and indeed saw that God kept His Word. God still keeps His Word today. And the things that we don't have are due to the fact that we haven't seized our moment. That's it! God is still good, and He is still passing out all kinds of stuff. But have you as an individual seized your moment?

Genesis 19:29 says:

> And it came to pass, when God destroyed the cities of the plain, that God remembered Abraham, and sent Lot out of the midst of the overthrow, when He over-threw the cities in which Lot had dwelt.

But God remembered. He remembered His friend.

A lot of people have been saved and delivered because of friends of God—people who pray and believe that God will give us our requests, our petitions, our prayers. You must remember that if Abraham had not requested this from God, then Lot would have been wiped out, too. Why? Because Lot was becoming one of them.

You know that old saying is still true, "One rotten apple in the barrel will spoil the whole bunch." Why is that? I've never heard anyone say if you have a bunch of rotten apples, put one good one in there and it will turn them all good. I've yet to hear that. It's something about that rotten apple. It's something about those people whose hearts and spirits aren't right, and God doesn't want you around them. He needs you to separate yourself from them!

Now I did not say that you can't go back and help them, but you can't continue to circulate yourself around them. They will get in you. Hang around someone with a cold, and you'll start sneezing. But you were fine at first. It's something about it. You cannot go to the next level if you're still dealing with these people. There are people at your job who you know are troublemakers. I suggest you get away from them. Now you're caught up in all kinds of issues. You said this and you said that. And you're saying, "I didn't say that." But you hang around them. Get away from that. And I do mean that. Work. Family. Friends.

If you're going to the next level, you had better separate yourself. I didn't say you shouldn't continue to love them. I didn't say you shouldn't continue praying for them. But you had better separate yourself from all of this mess and all of this gossip. And you're wondering why you're going through this situation. You've gotten down in the valley. Stay up in the mountains. If no one is calling you "troubling," you're better off. If no one is visiting you with trouble, you're better off. It didn't seem like Abraham was complaining. He was up in the mountains. He could have gone down low to the valley. He said, "I know what comes with that when I go low. I don't dwell in valleys. I don't dwell in low places."

How about the ravens? The ravens dwelled in the mountains. Ravens dwelled with ravens. They dwell at the top. God wants to take you to the top if you're willing to seize your moment. I don't know what it is for you, but you know. Everyone knows what is in their heart. I believe that day when we get there to see Him face to face. The Bible says we're going to be crying and weeping. We'll be crying and weeping, first because of His goodness, His grace, and His mercy. Second, I'm positive He's going to say, "Why didn't you do this? Why didn't you do that? Didn't you hear Me speak to you? Why didn't you seize your moment?" And I think that's going to hurt. When you ask if you could have had all of that, and He replies, "Yes. Your season and your time were right there."

Let's move on to verse 30. "Then Lot went up out of Zoar and dwelt in the mountains." Yes, he finally went there. "Then Lot went up out of Zoar and dwelt in the mountains, and his two daughters were with him; for he was afraid to dwell in Zoar. And he and his two daughters dwelt in a cave."

Then (which means it took him some time) Lot finally went to the mountains. Have you ever noticed throughout your life somehow, some way, you find yourself going where you should have gone in the first place? You say, "I could have been here a long time ago if I would have seized my moment. I have delayed my life. I have delayed my blessings. If I had gone back, taken a stand on His Word, I would have been here a long time ago. I've wasted money. I've wasted time, jumping from job to job, church to church, relationship to relationship, doing this and that. I could have been here a long time ago."

Remember, the mountains are where God told Lot to go. When God speaks to you, He is telling you that your place, your destiny is now! But no, you're going to pick somewhere else and choose your own thing. But life has a way of keeping you in place. It says you're going to do this anyway. Now, you're forty, fifty, sixty, or seventy. You could have been blessed a long time ago, had you been obedient to the Word of God. But Lot finally gets there. He finally makes up in his mind to go to the mountain. But he didn't go, based on his own decision.

The scripture reads, "Then Lot went up out of Zoar and dwelt in the mountains, and his two daughters were with him; for he was afraid to dwell in Zoar." First of all, who told Lot to leave Zoar? You know—like those people who up and jump and quit a job. No one told you to leave that job, and now you don't have a job. No one told you to up and jump and leave that man or that woman. Who told you to do that? I didn't hear anything about God speaking to him like He spoke to Abraham. Did you see that in your Bible? Nobody told him to do that. Some people might call this walking on faith. But I disagree because he didn't have guidance from God. You know the things we do sometimes. We just up and jump and do something. Nobody told you to do that, unless God spoke to you. And if He did, then you do just that. He just up and jumped and left. Was that not the place he picked?

We want to give Satan credit for a lot of stuff that we do. We say things like, "I know it's just the devil fighting me."

No, it's you. You have been delaying your blessings. You have been delaying your life. You put yourself in lack. "The enemy is fighting me." No, you're beating yourself up pretty good because you have a hard head. The Word of God is speaking to you, but you do what you want to do. Abraham was in the mountains, not in a cave. Get to the mountains. Seize your moment. When God speaks to your heart and mind, don't delay. You could have had this a long time ago. I tell my son and daughter to do this or do that. The time is now! When they're obedient to my word, I have blessings already stored up for them.

When God told Lot to go to the mountains, when He gave him that vision, God had already made the provision. Everything was already connected and in place if he had gotten there. I tell my son, "Hey, clean this up. Do this. Do that." But he wants to go to dragging. That means he delays all that I have for him, not to mention the consequences that come along with it. Think about it; it's that simple. One hour, two hours, three hours. One day, two days, three days. One week, two weeks, three weeks. One month, two months, three months. Four years, five years, six years. Now he wants to finally do it, but he missed what I had for him.

Why would you want to delay that? God is speaking to you right now. Don't try to understand it. When I have my children do this or that, they can't understand the reason behind it all. Just as Isaiah 55:8–9 says, "For My thoughts are not your thoughts, nor are your ways My ways," says the LORD. For as the heavens are higher than the earth, so are My ways higher than your ways, and My thoughts than your thoughts." In other words, "It makes no sense to you. Trust Me on this, and then I will ask you to look back and you will see the marvelous work I've done in your life."

But you must seize the moment! But Lot lingered. He wasn't quite confident, which means he obviously lacked trust and did not seize his moment. That also allowed his wife to look back. This is for leaders. Remember Lot's wife looked back past him, which means she was in front. It was the fact that he did not seize the moment and get excited about the Word of God speaking into his life and make a move.

When God spoke to Abraham, he told Sarah, "Let's go." He took the lead, didn't he? He said, "Wherever God tells me to go, I'm going." (See Genesis 12:1, 4.) But not the nephew. Abraham seized the moment. When Abraham seized the moment, Abraham seized the blessings. It's connected. When God speaks to you, now is the time. Your blessing is all wrapped up in it. Don't try to understand it. Samuel asked Saul, "Is not obedience better than sacrifice?" (See 1 Samuel 15:22.) Are you willing to make a move and take a stand now? You know He spoke to you, but you want to delay it.

Had he taken charge, his wife would have gone with him. But since he wasn't sure, she wasn't sure. Then he chose his own path. God told him to go to the mountains, but he went to Zoar. He preferred going elsewhere. Then he asked God, "Is it not little?" Now keep in mind that Zoar is on the same plains as Sodom and Gomorrah. Zoar was going to get wiped out just like Sodom and Gomorrah. The same people who dwelled in Sodom and Gomorrah also dwelled in Zoar. That's why he was scared. The same people he tried to leave are the same people in the other place he chose. That's why he was struggling and scared. He went to the same people. God said, "Get away to the mountains." But he just moves across the street. He's in the same neighborhood, dealing with the same people.

Is your life still a mess, even though you have moved on and you are still dealing with the same kind of people? You're taking bad advice, doing those same things, because you're dealing with the same people. Get away from that. I know they're going to talk about you, but think about it, they're going to do that anyway. It doesn't hurt my feelings if my phone doesn't ring. It doesn't hurt my feelings if no one comes by. That's great. When you're in the mountains, that's what happens. Think about it, for you to get to the mountains, you have to travel a long way. It had better be something important to go to the mountains. Jesus went to the mountains for the transfiguration. Moses went to the mountains. Elijah went to the mountains, to the top.

That is where God wants to take you—to the top. Valley people do not go to the mountains. They dwell in low places like snakes, and always seem to come out after you kick over a rock in your life. Don't go where they are; let them come up to you. And if they are who they are, they will make it. If not, they will die out. You are better off.

From the Scriptures, it seems that Lot had lost his relationship with God. While Lot's family seemed to stop, Abraham's family seemed to grow and prosper. Why was that? His family stopped because he didn't seize his moment. He was not obedient to the word of God. Abraham, on the other hand, was just the opposite. God said go, he left. God said stay, he dwelled. He stayed blessed. As a matter of fact, he received the seed of all blessings, which came through him.

Lot became a hermit and dwelled in a cave, not reaching any other levels that God had for him in his life. Abraham, on the other hand, continued to stay blessed over and over. Think about what God has spoken to you in your life. Go back and take a stand, and then seize the moment!

For protection God is the only thing every man should stand under.

—ELLIS POWELL

Knowledge is knowing what to do, understanding is knowing why to do it, wisdom is knowing when to do it, and character is consistently doing it.

—ELLIS POWELL

An old key is worthless unlocking a new door.

—ELLIS POWELL

A new location cannot be found using an old map.

—ELLIS POWELL

Nothing can stop the man with the right mental attitude, but nothing on earth can help the man with the wrong mental attitude.

—THOMAS JEFFERSON

Nine

Don't Bring Old
Baggage

IF I MAY add a quick note here—it all starts with God. No one is here by accident. God is not a gambler, and He is not rolling the dice. None of us are here by chance! This is all strategically planned. He had you in mind from the beginning. God says this, "If you find me, you will find you." Many people fail to understand what their lives are all about. Why? Because they haven't found Him! "It is I that is in you. Only when you find Me, will I reveal you to you. You really don't know you that well. I've known you since the beginning. I can tell you about you, but you must find Me."

I don't know if you've realized it yet, but each chapter has been vital. You can see it in people's day-to-day life. We had "The Ravens Are Coming," and anyone who has been blessed by a job, an opportunity, money, food, transportation—it came through people. Those are the ravens that God chooses to bless you.

In order to get to the next level, we talked about "Don't Get Comfortable." Well, truly if you find that making your $10, $20, or $30 an hour or whatever that number may be, if you're OK with that number, then you're truly maxed at your level. You've said, "This is enough for me. I'm comfortable with the car I drive. I'm comfortable with the house I live in." Now, again, I did not say that you were not appreciative or content, but I'm saying don't get comfortable. Don't stop reaching for your full potential or striving for the best God has for you. It is your very thoughts that will hold you back. There is always more. I did not say anything about jealousy or greed. But if the opportunity is there and He opens the door, I think it is worthwhile to walk through it. If you're a line employee, I'm sure there is a management position available. If you're a manager, I'm sure there is a director's position there. If you're a director, I'm sure there is some type of VP position available. If you're a VP, I'm sure there is some sort of president position out there. If you want to be an entrepreneur and stop working for everybody else (and work for yourself), that's out there, too. There are always next levels if you decide not to get comfortable.

We also talked about "Don't Look Back." It is very hard to get to the next level if you keep looking back. If I keep walking and looking back, sooner or later I'm going to have an accident because I'm not aware of where I'm going. Yet, if I'm still connected to what's back there, I don't get a chance to get into what's in my future.

We went from there to "Looking Back Will Cost You." Sure it will cost you. It will cost you time and money. Both are very valuable. What I mean by value is that if I were to continue to stay concentrated and focused on my future, I am easily able to let go of my past. Wrong relationships and wrong opportunities, if you are not careful, will cost you. "Head to the Top" means head to the mountains, the top.

Be the best you, you can be. We need to stop trying to be what everyone else thinks we should be. If you're a Kim, don't be a Tina. If you're a Tina, don't be a Kim. God says, "I want the best Kim; if I wanted another Tina, I would have created another Tina." But a lot of people can't seem to find themselves because they haven't found God. He reveals you to you. But we're so busy trying to get approval from everyone else, except Him.

> "If you continue to do what you've always done, then you'll continue to get what you've always gotten."

So, once we get to the mountains, now what? This chapter is "Don't Bring Old Baggage." What do I mean by that? I mean, there are new jobs, new relationships, that we all have entered in, and we bring all of our old stuff with us. If you continue to find yourself saying things like, "I don't know why I keep going through all of this. Why do these things keep happening to me?" Well, I'm sure if you walk back and retrace your steps, you're doing the exact same stuff you did in your old job or your old relationship.

There is a saying that states, "If you continue to do

what you've always done, then you'll continue to get what you've always gotten." Don't bring all of your old baggage. If you have a new job, I suggest you forget all of those old habits you were doing at the old place. God has given you a new level. He has taken you to a new height, and these new people don't know anything about you. They only know what you show them. Why is that in every job you seem to get, it seems like everyone there is talking about you? It's you. Why is that with every relationship you seem to get in, these things seem to continue to happen to you? I'll give you the common denominator. It's YOU! You continue to say the same old stuff, think the same old thoughts, go to the same old places, and yet you expect something new.

Now, if my apartment was junky, I suggest I leave those bad habits there. It is hard to move into a new house when you've packed up all of your old furniture. The new place is going to be nasty, too. It's just that simple. The furniture I am speaking of is your habits, your thinking, and your doing. It is just a matter of time before your new place is going to look like your old place. And people from the outset are going to say, "Well, it didn't do God any good to bless you, because you haven't changed at all." And that is so true.

In order for you to get to the next level, you must forget about your past. Don't forget the valuable lesson you've learned from it, but forget the failures you may have had. If I'm married now, I can't hang out with my old single friends the way that I used to. If I do not disconnect myself from them, it is just a matter of time before I'll be back single, too. I must get to the next level. If I'm trying to be a manager or obtain some type of management position in my company, I have to disconnect my line level employee mentality.

Anyone who has been promoted from a level employee to management, the boss always pulls you to the side (I don't care who you are) and says, "You know you're in management now. You're going to have to watch your relationships. If you continue to be buddies with them, it is just a matter of time before your job will be very difficult, and you will no longer be in your position anymore." You say "But they're my friends, I have to continue to be with them." Well, you go on any way. You'll be back there with them. I promoted you because I saw something within you. I've taken you to the next level, but you decide to stay connected to the valley. So from the mountains, back to the valley you will go! The people we hang with are very, very influential. Whether it is for good reasons or bad, both impact our lives. I suggest you hang with whoever is going where you want to go or whoever is there to help and assist you in getting where you want to go.

Earlier I spoke about the individual who doesn't have a car and wants to go to a specific destination in life. That person, although not having a vehicle, still successfully reaches his or her destination. Why? Because they partnered with one who was traveling the same direction! Scripture states, two are better than one for when one falls the other is there to pick him up. (See Ecclesiastes 4:9–10.)

Never go after your dream alone! Always partner with someone who sees what you see, so when your vision sometimes through tiresome, hard work becomes blurry, they are there to help you see the big picture clearer. Instead of saying how can I get connected to that, many people with bad thoughts and negative mentalities will be envious and hateful of the people who are going to the next level. I see that you're not struggling financially—what are you doing? I see that your marriage seems to be going really well—what's working for you? I see you are excited about life—what is it? That sounds like a wise person. The foolish man, instead, just gets mad and angry. As a matter of fact, the foolish person gets so mad and bitter that he becomes poison. These persons never say anything good anymore, because they have disconnected themselves. There's a song that talks about needing others to survive. If my going to the next level is based on helping you get there, so be it.

In this chapter, we're going to talk about the two daughters of Lot. Earlier, we discussed Lot and his family. Later in life Lot finally made it to the place he should have been many years prior! He finally went where God had told him to go in the first place.

Many of us have delayed our years of the abundant life through fear, disobedience, or not recognizing the hand of God on our lives. But let me show you how this comes back to bite him. Genesis 19:31 says:

> Now the firstborn said to the younger, "Our father is old, and there is no man on the earth to come in to us as is the custom of all the earth."

I told you awhile back that if we're going to go to the next level, we must have the same mind-set that Paul, David, and Solomon had, of forgetting those former things.

Let me ask you a quick question here. Where did Lot

and his family first reside? They first resided in Sodom and Gomorrah, that wicked and evil place. That was the place where the girls grew up. As a matter of fact, when King Chedorlaomer captured them, Abraham came to rescue them and asked Lot, "Do you want to come back with me?" Lot said, "No, I'd rather go back to Sodom and Gomorrah."

Then God comes down and says, "I've heard the people's outcries, and I am here to destroy Sodom and Gomorrah for all of its evil and wickedness." He tells Lot to take his family and head to the mountains. What does Lot do? He basically tells God, "No, I'd rather go to a little small town called Zoar."

Zoar was no more than a sister city of Sodom and Gomorrah. I hope I'm painting a picture for you. One saying is, "If you don't watch yourself, you will become a by-product of your environment." If you're raised up in mess, you're going to be a mess. Why? Because you are going to get mess all in you.

I'm going to tell you right now, if a father is out in the streets doing all kinds of stuff, the chances are that the son is going to be the same way. The mother out there cursing, having no self-control and acting crazy, the chances are that the daughter is going to be the exact same way. Why? Because they have no choice. They are being reared up in that type of an environment, and these people see nothing wrong with what they're doing. I hear people say all of the time, "Well, my dad did it. Well, my mom did it." That doesn't make it right! I'm sure if you pulled them to the side they would tell you, "Don't do that. I was wrong. I was foolish and didn't know any better."

We need to be careful of who our children are hanging around. It's like the cuckoo bird that we talked about. If you don't raise your kids, the streets and the wicked world will. So many of these kids have so much "street" in them. They have so much hustle, sly, scheming ways in them. They have so much of what radio, television, Internet, and society at large has put in them. And we know who they are; that's the reason we want to know who's going to be there when our kids are invited to a function or something. We say things like, "I don't want my child around this boy because this boy will influence my child." "This little fast girl will influence my daughter." Notice, the scripture said that the older daughter told the younger daughter. We know about that. We've been kids and looked up to our older brother or our older cousin because they were heavily influential.

You must remember now, this older girl was raised up in Sodom. She was raised up in Gomorrah. She was raised up in Zoar. So this young girl was corrupted early in life by the society she was in. She was raised up in a wicked and evil society. So we see here in verse 31 that she has concocted a thought and said, "Hey, there aren't any men around here, so let's get our father drunk." It was her thoughts that were developed from her environment.

Men, protect your wives. If you notice that the women they hang around aren't right, I suggest you confront it. No, I didn't say go all crazy and go off. But say, "Hey Susie, Kim, Linda, or whomever it is, I don't think they have the same values and are after the same things that we're about." Sure, she'll get mad, but that is because you're about to separate them. Women, do the same thing for your husbands. If they are hanging around some Casanova who is still going in the fast lane of life, partying, club scenes, and still chasing women, then you better believe that they are in that environment. If your husband says, "Oh, I'm not like that." Well, what is it that draws and connects you to them? There has to be something within you that connects you with these individuals.

Protect your children. Kids are walking around with their pants hanging down and saying all kinds of stuff, I suggest that you seclude your children from these kids. If you won't raise your children, these other kids will. It will get in them, for sure. They are building more penitentiaries, more "troubled youth" facilities. They can't keep up with the AIDS clinics needed!

The epidemic is spreading like wildfire. Sure, I may have to stay up a little late and talk to them a little more. I may have to chastise or discipline a couple of more times, but I cannot afford to lose them to a world that devours the young. Where would they go? I thought you were the mom. I thought you were the dad. "Well, since he won't listen to me, he has to go." Well, you know if he won't listen to his own parents, I don't think he's going to do too much with Aunt Betty and Grandma.

> We have to fight for what God has given to us!

We have to fight for what God has given to us! He did not cast us aside, so why do we cast our own aside? So this older daughter was convincing her younger sister to do something wicked and evil. Although they finally moved to the mountains, they were already raised up in a wicked and evil environment. When your children say,

"Well, Mom, can I just run here with this person?" You had better check and see who "this person" is. If you don't check, "this person" is slowly influencing your family. I hear parents say all the time, "Boy, I don't even know who you are anymore." That's right, you don't because he's changed. Someone else has been influencing him and planting more thoughts.

Although they made it to the mountains, this older daughter brought her old baggage with her. A lot of us have been hurt in relationships, and now we cannot keep a new relationship. Why? Because we're bringing all of that old stuff that was done to us into the new relationship.

Leave that in the past! You must take on the attitude that, "Sure, maybe I got fired or did something wrong, but I will not do that on my next job. I will leave those old thoughts and old habits. Sure I used to act crazy and fight with my spouse, and now we're divorced, but I will not do that in my next marriage. Sure, I used to drink and get loud and act crazy, but I will not do that again!" Remember, you cannot change anything you are not willing to confront. I will leave that old stuff in the past.

So she goes on to say in verse 31, "Our father is old and there is no man on the earth to come into us." She has convinced the younger girl that there are no men on earth anymore. They are in a cave, and they just left Zoar, and obviously there were people there, but she has convinced her younger sister that they will not have any kids if they don't do this.

Now, how many times have people of bad influence influenced us? There are some that influence us by saying things like, "Now, if you don't do this, you are not cool. If you don't this, you are not right. If you don't do this...if you don't do this..." It's always someone who is older than we are, someone whom we respect, trust, and feel comfortable with.

The younger one wasn't old enough yet to have enough wickedness in her. She wasn't like the oldest one, but she had a relationship with her sister. We have to be careful about that. It doesn't matter if it is your sister, your brother, your mom, or your dad, because if they don't know Christ, then I don't know. You should still love and respect them, but if they're headed down the wrong road, I suggest that you don't follow them. I am sure that this younger girl did not want to lose a relationship with her sister.

A lot of us are like that. We've been talked into doing some stuff. Even when we are left by ourselves, it seemed that our own thoughts coerced us. Well, how do you get talked in to doing some stuff? You are able to line up to what He says and say, "That's not what He says, and I'm not doing it." If God could send Moses out into Median, to Jethro who had all of those daughters who were not married, He could send a man to where Lot's daughters were. But obviously Lot's older daughter didn't have that relationship with God.

Genesis 19:32 reads, "Come, let us..." Have you ever noticed that wicked people always wants you to join in? The older daughter could have just done it herself. She didn't have to get her baby sister involved. She didn't have to corrupt her sister. A lot of us are by-products of people causing much harm and pain in our lives. The younger sister had no desire to do that. Someone got to her. It was her big sister.

Sometimes, in our own house, we have to watch out for those big sisters who might get you to do things that you would never do. I am sure we've all said that to ourselves: "You know, I thought I would never do that. I thought I would never say that." The older sister could have just said to herself, "I'm going to go ahead and get my father drunk and do this dirt and that's it!" She could have told her sister, "You don't have to do this; you're better than me. You weren't raised up like I was."

You know people love to put the blame on where they were raised. "I was raised in poverty, and this is just how I am." No, this is how you accepted yourself to be. I said earlier, if you find Him, you will find *you*!

The problem is that you are lost! You are trying to navigate your own self. So Lot's older daughter was corrupted. You can tell that her thoughts were corrupted by the words she spoke.

You see, when you think bad thoughts, your heart gets corrupted. You begin to speak bad things, and you are moved to do some bad things. *Watch out!* So she thought it, she felt it, she spoke it, and you better believe that she is about to do it! Foolish!

We better watch out for these people, because if they say bad things, they're thinking bad thoughts. Old stuff. So the older daughter said:

> Come, let us make our father drink wine, and we will lie with him, that we may preserve the lineage of our father.
>
> —GENESIS 19:32

See, they always throw a little something in there. "Let's go and steal this because we've had it hard our whole lives." See how they throw that in there. "Mother really deserves this; let's go in there and take this real quick, because she needs something nice, too." They throw that in. They try to throw in a just cause to do the wrong act! You can't get me to believe that God would tell you to do wrong for something that's right. "I had to go steal, my family was hungry." No, you could have gone to another brother or sister. So Lot's older daughter tried to con her young sister and say, "We have to have kids because that's what we're supposed to do. So we need to do this wrong to justify our means." This older sister was already wicked and corrupted.

Verse 33 reads, "So they made their father drink wine." I just love that part that says, "So they made their father." How are you going to make your daddy do something? "So they made their father drink wine that night. And the firstborn went in and lay with her father, and he did not know when she lay down or when she arose."

I don't drink. That's a personal thing for me. I don't care how bad my children came in and said, "Hey, Dad, why don't you sit down and rest your feet and grab you a glass or two?" You can't get me to do that. Let me show you how corrupt the older daughter was. She knew her dad couldn't handle drinking. For this man to get drunk and not know that she came in or went out, he was certainly not sober. He said, "I don't remember anything. Did you come in here last night?"

This man must have drunk some bottles or buckets or barrels. He didn't know anything. The thing is that she must have known that he would do this. Her plan, the entire time, was to get him drunk. And to plan to get him drunk, she must have known that he would start drinking.

Listen carefully: Satan knows your weakness. He will use them against us. He knows you can't resist the nice cars and the shopping mall. He knows what works on you because it always has worked on you. Until you're able to stand up to it and stand on God's Word, you're in trouble.

Lot's older daughter knew it worked on him. Now again, the wickedness and evilness are no more than characteristics of Satan. Now the child was good. It's her spirit that was bad. "I know Daddy can't handle liquor, so I'm going to get him drunk." Yet, I look at him and all of us.

Whatever your weakness is, I suggest that you be quick about identifying it. Don't ignore it. It will take you out. You're trying to lose weight and know you can't control your eating; I suggest you start dealing with it. You're married and have a lust for a whole lot of women, because that person is still in you; I suggest you deal with it. Our spouses and mates know the other "person." That is why they go off the deep end. In other words, that scenario I just told you about when the husband still has some attitude in him and the wife sees him surrounded by some beautiful women—the wife goes off the deep end. She knows that he's in a situation that he can't control. The husband knows the wife can't handle getting caught up in a lot of mess and gossip and he finds out that she's on the phone with Sherry. The husband goes off. He knows she can't handle it. We were in this thing two years ago dealing with this, and now you're back in it. You know you can't handle this. She's married to an alcoholic, and they're at a wedding reception. He says, "I'm just going to have one drink." She's going to sound off. "You know you can't handle this. He is using this to break us up. He's using this to take us out." That's what he used on the older daughter to take them out. He knew Lot couldn't handle drinking, so that's what he used on him. We all still have some weaknesses.

The worst thing you can do is ignore your weaknesses and act like you don't have any. The wise person recognizes it and deals with it immediately. To the man who drinks, I suggest he get a glass of punch quickly and stop trying to hang around those people who are still drinking. He can't handle it! To the man who still has a flirtatious spirit and is getting a lot of compliments from a group of women, I suggest he get out of that quickly! You can't handle it! I'm just trying to make this plain. Satan knew he could take him out with that drinking, but let me show you how we don't learn. So that was verse 33.

Genesis 19:34 states, "It happened on the next day..." Although Satan flees, he will return. Oh, he is going to come back. He only comes back with the same thing. He knows it works, so he tries again. You didn't have a drink this time, but he'll invite you to another social gathering that will be serving alcohol. He comes to tempt, and we must recognize him. I know who is behind this. We think that he comes through individuals, but that is only one of his vehicles. His main vehicle is right in you! What about the time he drinks and there is no one around? No one coerced him. It got into his thought pattern. He says, "One won't hurt," but all of a sudden he's finding a beer here and there. Now he's hiding drinks in the mailbox and in the backseat of the truck. All of a sudden, his paycheck money is a little short. Now you can even hardly find him. It goes on and on and on.

Verse 34 states, "It happened on the next day that the firstborn said to the younger, 'Indeed I lay with my father last night.'" Here we go. I told you, he couldn't do anything by himself. He needs us. The devil has no power. He needs us to participate. He told Eve, "That fruit sure looks good, doesn't it? You should get that. You should have that." Eve says, "You think so?" He has no power. The power he has is the power we give him, which means we have power. He has no power.

Lot's older daughter comes back to convince the younger girl by saying, "'Indeed I lay with my father last night; let us make him drink wine tonight also, and you go in and lie with him, that we may preserve the lineage of our father.' Then they made their father drink wine that night also. And the younger arose and lay with him, and he did not know when she lay down or when she arose" (Gen. 19:34–35). I'm shaking my head, too. Lot learned nothing.

Did you not learn from your last mistake? Did you not learn from your last relationship? Did you not learn from your last job? He comes back the next night and does the exact same thing. Why? He did not deal with his weakness. I told you, if your wife went out with her friend and liked it, she's going back out. He's hanging out with his buddy at the café. Watch out, he's going back! If he goes back, you had better deal with him right then. Otherwise, he is gone! It is going to be hell getting him back. It is going to be tough getting her back. It's the same way with the kids. He's going to come back and tempt you with the same thing that worked the last time. Why? Paul says,

"Because you have given him a foothold in your life." Then we come back and say, "I don't know why I keep going through this." You've given him power. He has no power. He needs to try to convince you and coerce you into doing wrong. That's how it works. He has no power. Lot made five mistakes. He made five bad choices.

1. He separated from Abraham (anyone who is righteous with God and whose life is blessed, I suggest you stay connected). Notice this. As long as he was with Abraham, he was blessed. As long as you're with God, you will be blessed.

2. God had rescued him when King Chedorlaomer had captured him, and he went back to the same place God brought him out of. Why do we go back to the same mess God brought us out of? "I'm not going to take him back anymore." OK, it's all right. You're going back to the same mess God freed you from.

3. God told Lot to head to the mountains, and he said "No, just take me to a nearby city." There you can see that he refused to separate himself from unrighteousness. It got in him.

4. Lot left Zoar without consulting God. No one told him to leave. Was that not the place he asked for? What I mean by this, is you know how people get married and say, "God gave me this man." But they jump up and divorce the man without consulting God. You asked for him or her or this job, but now you're going to jump up and leave. That was Lot's mistake. Notice, had Lot not left Zoar, he would have never been secluded and his daughters would have never done what they did. It's all connected.

One thing leads to another. It is called "bringing old baggage."

5. Drinking. Lot did not deal with his weakness. Whatever it may be, we all have some weaknesses. What makes us wise and stronger is that we have identified our weaknesses and know how to deal with them. What are your weaknesses? You can take the cow out of the country, but you cannot take the country out of the cow. He got them out of there, but it was already in them. We must continue to perfect and protect our relationships with ourselves, our spouses, our children, our family members, and our friends. It is vital if you're going to the next level.

I will study and get ready and perhaps my chance will come.

—ABRAHAM LINCOLN

When your heart decides the destination, your mind will design the map to reach it.

—ELLIS POWELL

Therefore, do not cast away your confidence, which has great reward.

—HEBREWS 10:35, NKJV

For we walk by faith, not by sight.

—2 CORINTHIANS 5:7, NKJV

Jesus said to him, "If you can believe, all things are possible to him who believes."

—MARK 9:23, NKJV

Chapter 10

GO WITH
EXPECTATIONS

I DIDN'T WANT TO end the book without a chapter on expectations. Understand, to have a mind-set of expectations will require the two *Cs*. The two *Cs* are confidence and commitment. The way you have confidence is realizing you are not alone in your journey of going to the next level. My suggestion to you, one that has proven successful for me, is partnering with someone that has a bit more power, riches, knowledge, and wisdom than us all. My ultimate business partner is God Himself. He has given mankind His Word (Jesus), to all that want to partner with Him. All you have to do is believe in His Word and you enter into His new covenant or contract/agreement.

God wants to invest in your life, business, family, and

dreams! Now understand, I am talking about the Creator of the universe, who made all things and has the perfect plans and timing. One who owns all the silver and gold, the earth, and all the inhabitants in it. He has charge over all the angels and therefore provides you with all the protection you need from any outside problems. He knows all, so therefore you have access to the greatest wise counsel ever!

Trust me, Wall Street doesn't stand a chance with Him! God holds the future in His hands, so you have comfort knowing your partner knows what tomorrow holds for you. He believes in reaping and sowing, and He believes in multiplying the little assets of His business partners and bringing forth thirty, forty, sixty, one hundred times as much as they had before! God is truly your long-term investment. The stock market average return is not even close to the yield of return He brings! God loves to work with people who are willing to invest and believe in Him. He has a portfolio that's astounding and a reference list that dates back over several thousand years. All of His deals are guaranteed, because He never goes back on His Word.

No matter how things look or seem to be going wrong or tough in your life, business, job, marriage, family, body, or mind, He said He would never leave you, abandon you, or run out on you. Now that is the type of partner that will give me that confidence, knowing whatever happens my partner will back me up. So now, I say, "Let us make history together. Let us create something new that has not been created." You see, I have confidence in my partner, and my partner has confidence in me! For I know that I can do all things through Him because He is with me! To have confidence, you must be willing to confide in your partner, who has a vested interest in your life, one who believes in your dreams and your visions.

Sometimes it is difficult to find someone of this caliber and character, because they can't see what you see, unless, just maybe, they gave you the dream in the first place. Follow me here! Let's discuss your dreams and aspirations. Did you just pick it out of thin air, or was there or is there something that has been pulling inside of you? And if it is pulling, then what is it attracted to? It's like a magnet that seems to keep drawing you along. Is it something that when someone mentions it you get all roused up? Is there someone whom you admire and respect who is already doing what you want to do? What is the urge that seems to nag at your subconscious?

God is the soil, the source, and the giver of all things if you are willing to plant or invest in Him. In time and in your season He will allow you to bring forth fruit.

Could it be your destiny that was placed in your future trying to find its place, and only you hold the key? Is your destiny like a lost bird trying to find its way home, and you, your life, are its home? Could your destiny be like a baby in its mother's womb growing and has not yet reach full term yet? If so, who placed the seed in you? *Hmm!* This is something to think about.

As I see it, God has already done some investing in us all; could it be that He is waiting on His return or profit? Just like a company, not only does the board reap much gain and benefits, but all the stockholders do as well.

Have you considered the dreams or visions you've had?

Have you invested in bringing those things to pass? This will be the best 401K you can ever invest in! Why? Because you can never max out this fund, and the owner, being God, will match you at 100 percent. James 4:8 states that as you draw near to God He draws near to you, which means when I move, He moves. So start investing in your life and dreams. You are closer to retirement than you think! Let God go over your portfolio and put your mind at ease. A dream comes through much activity, but no dream *is impossible*. The hardest thing about a dream is trying to see it. You see, if you can't see it in your mind, it doesn't exist. But if you can, then it is *REAL*. All you have to do is begin working on it!

I hope I have shown you that if you are willing to make the first step, your business partner will make the next step. Consider your talents and abilities. Why am I good at this? Why is it that I just know this? These are gifts or investments God has given to you to work on and use to go to the next level. You see, your talents are already blessed and approved by Him, and they are tied to your wealth and prosperity.

Fear not, no matter what things seem to be. The world is ready to make room for you because you are one of a kind. You are unique, special, and bona fide. The scripture states that your gift will make room for you. (See Proverbs 18:16.) It also states it will set you among great people. If you can muster up enough courage and confidence, trust me, people will seek you out because of your gift, talents, and dreams. Please, for your future's sake, work on your talent, gift, and dreams. They will bring you so much happiness that you will not comprehend.

I know you are saying, "How can I look past my situations? There seems like there is no way this can happen." Understand, your situation *is not* real. Why? Because it is subject to change. Think on this: the only thing that has to be real is something that cannot change and stays in its pure and original state all the time. That's *God!* Therefore, cast your cares, worries, and doubts on Him, for He cares for you and wants to see you succeed in life. Peter wrote, "Casting all your care upon Him, for He cares for you" (1 Pet. 5:7). God wants

> Think on this: the only thing that has to be real is something that cannot change and stays in its pure and original state all the time. That's *God!*

you to have life and have it more abundantly. So I encourage you to include Him in all your plans and watch what happens. Now you can start to expect things because you have allowed Him to direct your path, and you are not leaning on your own understanding.

You see, God created the universe and aligned it and set it in place. When you partner with God, the entire universe is at your disposal; it will respond to you and will align all the right things and people in your path—just as the solar system is positioned perfectly and the earth revolves receiving all that it needs to survive and be effective. The earth continues to turn and use the sun, moon, and stars for its benefit. You have to become like the earth and get to turning and expecting things to come your way. Trust me; it will not be luck, chance, or coincidence, but it will be God using the universe to respond to your request.

Wow! That really takes the pressure off.

Illustration: When a farmer plants a seed in the ground and continues to water and fertilize it, is he surprised when it grows over time and brings forth fruit? Of course not! He has been expecting it the whole time. He did his part and allowed the soil, the source, and the giver to do its part. Note: God is the soil, the source, and the giver of all things if you are willing to plant or invest in Him. In time and in your season He will allow you to bring forth fruit.

Notice in the illustration the farmer had his part to do. He had to keep watering and fertilizing the seed. Now that takes the second *C*, commitment. You will have to stay focused and make whatever your goal or dream a *priority*. Without commitment, the seed would die before it even had a chance to break ground. You see, no matter what you are believing for, you have to keep watering your seed (dream). The most important stage is when the seed is trying to develop some roots underground.

The roots are very important later in life. Why? Because when things get tough, the tree will have to rely on its roots. There will be some tough times and conditions, such as dry seasons, bad weather, pestilence attack, and strong winds; all these things will come along and affect the tree life and its growth. The dry seasons are when it seems you can't catch a break and no rain has come. The rain is a sign of relief, blessings, and good times. The bad weather is when there will be unforeseen occurrences that happen in life such as death of a loved one, sickness, divorce, family relationships, injury, or financial loss. The pest attacks are just that. People in your life that only come to eat off of your fruit before they are ripe or simply bring germs or fungus—negative comments or problems that will hinder you to bloom and succeed. The strong winds, believe it or not, are heaven sent. Why? Because God controls the wind; therefore, it is sent—in a good way. It is the winds that show you if your tree is rooted and can handle what comes its way. The winds toss the tree to and fro, which causes the tree to entrench itself deeper and deeper by its roots. Again, it is the roots that determine its survival and how long it will last. But it's the soil that determines how many branches and how tall it gets. These things will happen in your life, but don't worry, because they can only *delay* your destiny, not deny it! You will recover! You must continue on watering (believing) in your dream or goal that God has given you. If not, your thirst and desire will never be quenched.

Then you must fertilize it. That requires action on your part to keep putting forth effort to bring it to pass. Scripture states, "Without faith it is impossible to please Him [God]" (Heb. 11:6). This is truly the missing secret ingredient. That combination, my friend, along with trusting in the soil is faith! That is truly the miracle that will grow any seed! Get it? Miracle Grow! You see, that's why a farmer uses fertilizer (which is chemical nutrients). That will enhance or increase the fertility of the soil. The faith (fertilizer) in God (the soil) will produce a fertile land (life). In other words, a fruitful, productive, and rich life you will start to have once you have followed these particular steps. But you must stay committed to it.

Scripture also states that faith without works is dead and that I will show you my faith by my works. (See James 2.) Yes, you will have to put your work where your mouth is. I believe an old saying goes something like that.

I remember growing up as a child watching a cartoon show called *GI Joe*. At the end of each episode, GI Joe would say, "Knowing is half the battle." Boy, was he right! Knowing is half the battle, because the other half is *doing* it! For many people who have said, "I prayed and prayed and prayed," once again, let's all learn from GI Joe! You have done the first half.

It's like a football game at halftime. You still have a whole second half to go! So come out of the locker room and hit the field! I never said it would be easy, but it is simple. There are no tricks to the trade. Success, being rich, and being happy are simple, but obtaining them will require much work and discipline. If you are willing to do it, then you are certainly within reason to receive it.

> Knowing is half the battle, because the other half is *doing* it!

When you step out on faith, know and understand you have God's Word—that's your policy, provision, and protection. As we move to the next level, I didn't want to end this book without an opportunity to offer all who want to partner with the Ultimate Business Partner (God) through Jesus Christ. There is truly no next level without Him!

I ask that you retrieve from any wrongdoing (repent/ apologize)! This is your first half. Believe (in Him that was sent—His Word). Receive (salvation/eternal life)! This halftime, go and achieve (the best life you can have)! This is the second half! Enjoy the second half and the rest of a great game!

Continue to climb to the top, and help many who are on your path. Please watch who you step on and climb over on your way there. For the old saying is so true, the same folks you see going up are the same ones you will see coming down.

See you at the top of your mountain! I look forward to the day of His return when we all will be *Going to the Next Level!*

To Contact the Author

www.ellisdpowell.com
ellis.powell@thedailybread.org